Professional
TENNIS DRILLS

D066096*4

Professional
TENNIS DRILLS

75 Drills to Perfect Your Strokes,
Footwork, Conditioning,
Court Movement, and Strategy

LEWIS BREWER
in cooperation with the
UNITED STATES TENNIS ASSOCIATION

Illustrations by
GROVER'S MILLS GRAPHICS

Charles Scribner's Sons • New York

Charles Scribner's Sons
Macmillan Publishing Company
866 Third Avenue, New York, N.Y. 10022
Collier Macmillan Canada, Inc.

Library of Congress Cataloging in Publication Data
Brewer, Lewis.
Professional tennis drills.

Bibliography: p.
1. Tennis—Training.   I. United States Tennis
Association.   II. Title.
GV1002.9.T7B74   1985   796.342′2   85-2066
ISBN 0-684-18298-X

Macmillan books are available at special discounts for bulk purchases
for sales promotions, premiums, fund-raising, or educational use.
For details, contact:

Special Sales Director
Macmillan Publishing Company
866 Third Avenue
New York, N.Y. 10022

10 9 8 7 6

Printed in the United States of America

TABLE OF CONTENTS

ACKNOWLEDGMENTS

A number of coaches contributed drills to this book. Without their cooperation this book would not have been possible:

David Benjamin
Princeton University

Nick Bollettieri
Nick Bollettieri Tennis Academy

Gayle Godwin
USTA Junior Federation Cup Coach

Chuck Kriese
Clemson University

Ann Lebedeff
University of Arizona

Doug MacCurdy
Director of Development
International Tennis Federation

Steve Stefanki
USTA Junior Davis Cup Coach

Larry Tabak
USTA Special Projects Coordinator

INTRODUCTION

Virtually everyone who plays tennis wants to improve. Yet most tennis players are not quite sure how to become better players. They may know that practice has something to do with improving their games, but they don't know how to practice. Very few people know how to organize a practice session. Furthermore, few players are able to devise practice routines. This book is for all tennis players who have these problems.

This is a book of tennis drills. It is not an instructional book. These drills assume you are familiar with proper form and correct grips, and will help strengthen and reinforce such skills. Drills are routines that allow players to hit a large number of balls in a short period of time, and thus help them use their court time more efficiently and effectively. The practice routines described in this book will help players of all levels structure their practices better.

This book is divided into three main chapters. The first chapter includes drills that will reinforce proper stroke production and allow players to groove their shots. The second chapter describes drills that will help improve two areas that are critical to winning tennis: court movement and physical conditioning. The third chapter describes drills that will allow players to practice situations that occur frequently in a tennis match.

If you have never drilled before, the best way to start is to set aside a specific period of time that will be devoted to practice with a partner of similar ability. When drilling, unless the purpose of the drill is to hit winners, your goal should be to keep the ball in play. Therefore, balls should be hit with a medium pace. Drilling should also be done in a pressure-free environment. Don't keep score or compare your efforts with your partner's. Concentrate on the task at hand and you will benefit from your time on the court.

Each drill in this book includes an explanation and illustration which will make it easy for you and your partner to follow. Although most of the drills are for two or four players, some group drills are included for the benefit of coaches and large groups or families.

Although drilling will help your game, there is a point of diminishing return. Your practice time should not be solely composed of drilling. Players who do nothing but drill tend to lose the competitive edge necessary to win matches. You must be prepared to include some practice sets in your tennis schedule. It is important for players to learn how to compete, and this can be done best by playing practice matches.

Organizing a practice is not as difficult as it might seem. Before you map out your practices, you should establish a set of goals for your practice. For example, if your goal is to improve your level of play, you should be prepared to schedule at least three practices a week. If your goal is simply to maintain your current level, one or two sessions a week should be sufficient.

Regardless of your level of play, each practice session should include technique drills, conditioning drills, and match situation drills. You should vary the drills in each practice session to avoid becoming bored by doing the same drills over and over. There are enough drills in each chapter to help you do this.

If you are a tournament player, you should practice at least one hour per session. A typical workout should include about ten minutes of technique drills, twenty minutes of conditioning drills, and thirty minutes of match play drills. If you can schedule more than an hour per session, simply increase the time spent on each type of drill. One of your practice sessions should be solely devoted to match play.

If you are an inexperienced player, you need to devote more practice time to technique drills. A good practice session should include thirty minutes of technique drills, fifteen minutes of conditioning drills, and fifteen minutes of match situation drills. You should also allow one day a week for match play.

One of the biggest mistakes any player can make is to devote practice time to working only on his or her weaknesses. Good players win matches because their strengths are better than their opponent's strengths. You should be sure that while trying to improve your weaknesses you maintain the strong points of your game.

This book was prepared with the cooperation of the United States Tennis Association, the governing body of tennis in the United States. The USTA is dedicated to helping more people discover the lifetime benefits of tennis, and to improving the tennis experience of those who play. For more information on programs offered by the USTA write:

UNITED STATES TENNIS ASSOCIATION
Education and Research Center
729 Alexander Road
Princeton, NJ 08540

1 REINFORCING FUNDAMENTALS

One of the main reasons why many players don't play as well as they would like is faulty stroke production. One leading tennis coach has called tennis a series of emergencies. For example, if you have a weak backhand and your opponent constantly hits the ball to your backhand, you are obviously faced with a series of emergencies. How well you respond to these emergencies determines how often you will win. If players concentrated on developing fundamentals, such as sound stroke production and proper balance, they could avoid many of the emergencies that occur during a match. The drills in this chapter will help you work on developing sound fundamentals.

General technique drills should be a part of every player's practice session. When you have to hit that down-the-line passing shot on an important point, a factor that will determine whether or not you will make the shot is how often you have drilled that particular shot. Tournament players will not have to devote as much practice time to these drills, but an inexperienced player should reserve about half of his or her practice time to work on technique. There is no set period of time to devote to the drills in this chapter. You should be your own judge of how much time to spend with each drill. If you and your partner are happy with a drill, then you can continue it for as long as you like. On the other hand, if you become bored with a drill, you should stop and try another one.

FOREHANDS CROSSCOURT

PLAYERS: 2

DRILL: This is a general technique drill for forehands. Every tennis player has done this drill at some time or other. It is a time-tested drill that will benefit every player. Both players A and B start at the baseline and hit only crosscourt forehands. The goal of the drill is to keep the ball in play to develop balance and control.

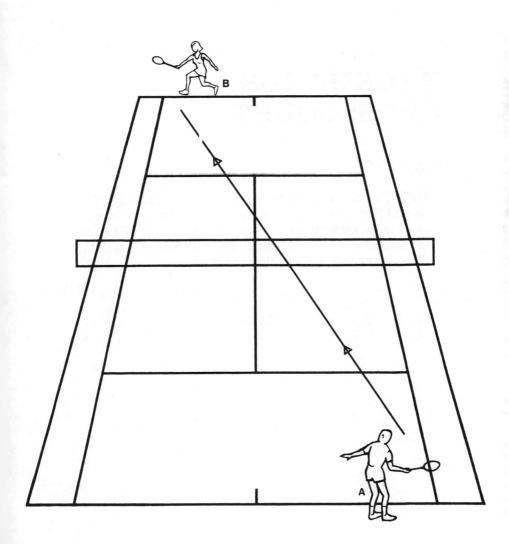

Forehands Crosscourt

BACKHANDS CROSSCOURT

PLAYERS: 2

DRILL: This drill is the same as the previous drill except players A and B are now hitting backhands. In addition to keeping the ball in play, this is the time to concentrate on your form. You should try to turn your shoulders as early as you can, stay on balance, and have a complete follow-through.

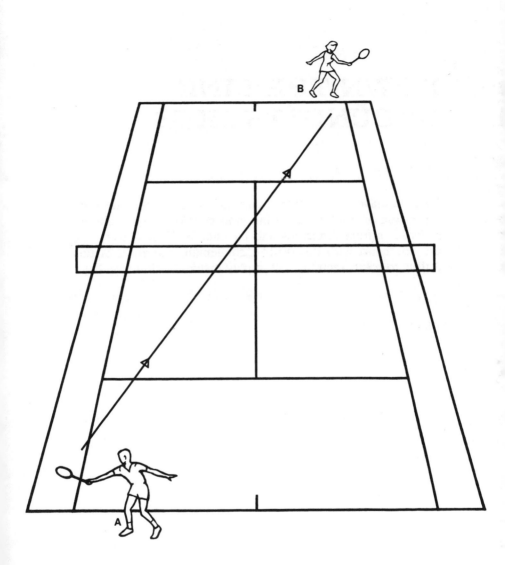

Backhands Crosscourt

DOWN-THE-LINE GROUNDSTROKES

PLAYERS: 2 or 4

DRILL: Players A and B try to hit the ball down the line, concentrating on footwork, timing, and control. Players should alternate hitting forehands and backhands. Four players can use one court with this drill. A challenging variation of this drill is to try to keep the ball in play inside the doubles alley.

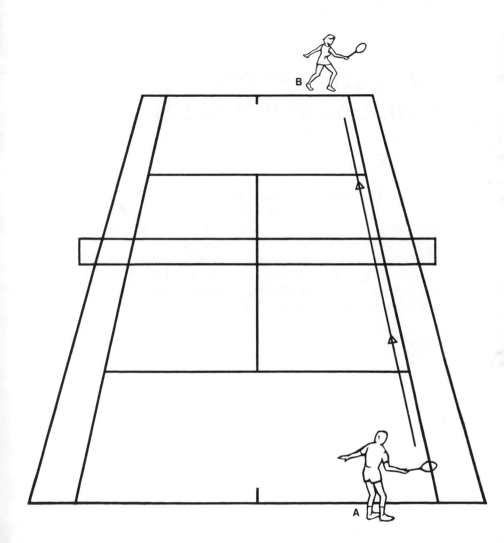

Down-the-line Groundstrokes

FIGURE EIGHT GROUNDSTROKES

PLAYERS: 4

DRILL: The purpose of this drill is to alternate hitting crosscourt and down the line. Player B starts the drill by hitting crosscourt to Player C. Player C then hits the ball down the line to Player A. Player A then hits crosscourt to Player D, and D returns the ball down the line to B. The goal of the drill is to keep one ball in play for as long as possible. The players should change periodically so that each has a chance to hit the ball crosscourt and down the line.

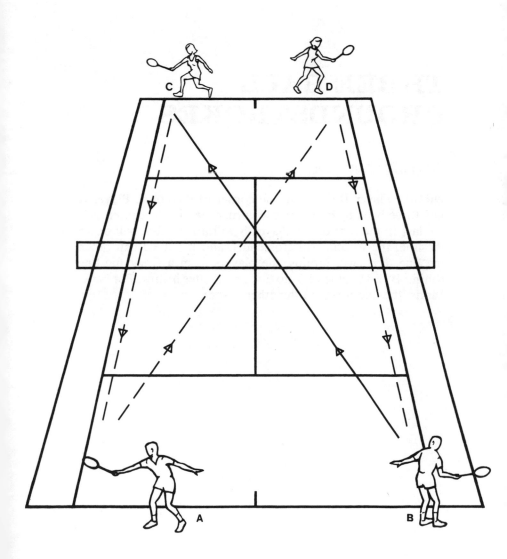

Figure Eight Groundstrokes

THREE-BALL GROUNDSTROKES

PLAYERS: 2 or more

DRILL: Player B starts in one corner of the court. Player A hits three balls to B; one in the corner, one in the center, and the last in the far corner. Player B will hit the first ball down the line, the second ball crosscourt, and the third ball down the line. For large groups, the players form a single-file line behind B and should pick up three balls after hitting. For backhands, the line forms in the other corner.

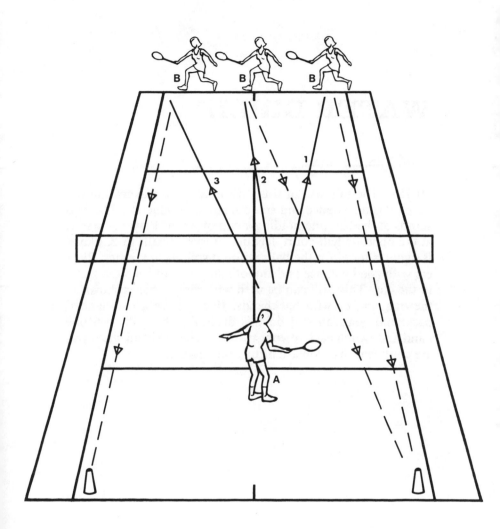

Three-ball Groundstrokes

WATER DRILL

PLAYERS: 2 or more

DRILL: The purpose of this drill is to have players concentrate on good balance and smooth stroke production. Player B stands at the baseline holding a cup of water. Player A stands at the opposite half-court, feeding a series of balls to B. Player B's goal is to return the balls without spilling any water. Players with good balance and smooth strokes will keep the water in the cup. This drill can be used with forehands, as shown in the diagram, or with backhands. If you have a two-handed backhand, you can still do this drill. Try the drill with one hand and switch back to your two-handed backhand when you are confident that you are hitting on balance.

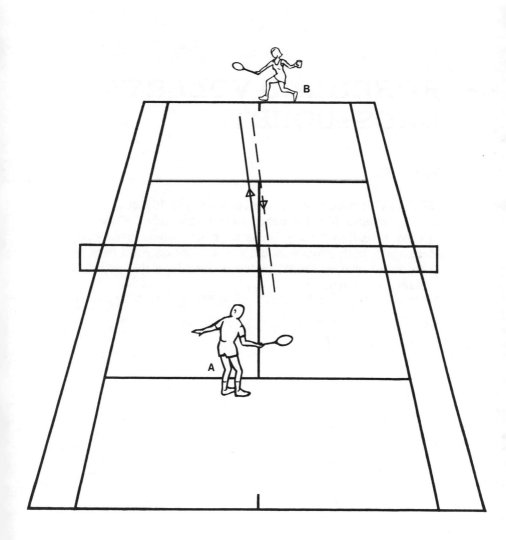

Water Drill

FOREHAND VOLLEYS CROSSCOURT

PLAYERS: 2

DRILL: This is another basic technique drill. Player B stands at the net and hits forehand volleys crosscourt. Player A returns the ball by hitting forehand groundstrokes crosscourt. Here again, both players should concentrate on good balance and control. Players should switch frequently so that each has a chance at the net.

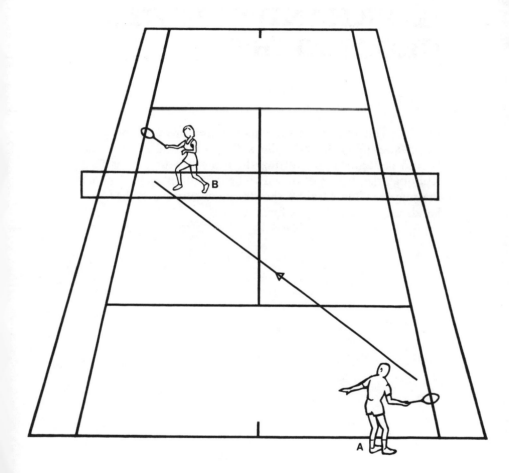

Forehand Volleys Crosscourt

BACKHAND VOLLEYS CROSSCOURT

PLAYERS: 2

DRILL: This drill is the same as the previous drill except the emphasis is on backhand volleys. Player B starts at the net and should concentrate on hitting the volleys with proper form. Although the drill is designed to benefit the player at the net, the player at the baseline should make sure his or her backhands are hit with proper form.

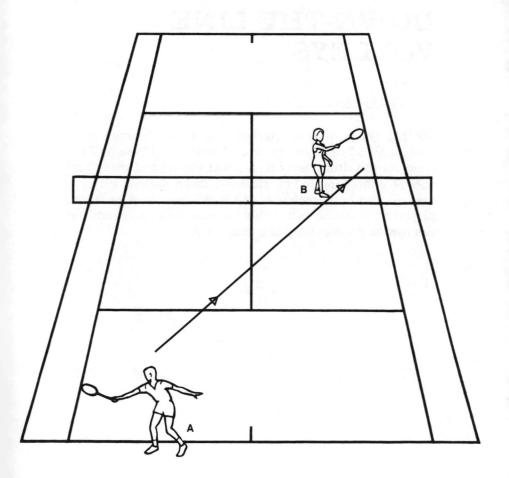

Backhand Volleys Crosscourt

DOWN-THE-LINE VOLLEYS

PLAYERS: 2 or 4

DRILL: The purpose of this drill is to practice hitting volleys straight ahead or down the line. Players should use half the court for this drill. Player B stands at the net and tries to hit volleys, either forehand or backhand, down the line. Player A may also hit both forehands and backhands. As a variation, players can limit the drill to either forehands or backhands and can use the doubles alley as a target area.

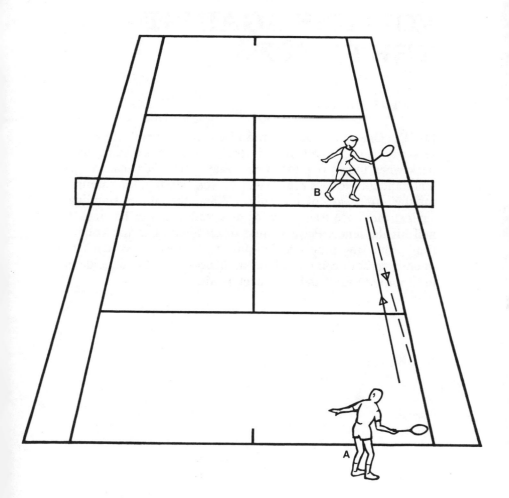

Down-the-line Volleys

VOLLEYS AGAINST THE FENCE

PLAYERS: 2 or more

DRILL: One of the most common mistakes when hitting volleys is swinging too much. This drill gives players instant feedback when they swing too much. Player B stands against the fence and hits volleys with Player A, who stands at the baseline on the same side of the court. When the player standing against the fence tries to swing at a volley, his or her racket will hit the fence. Players must reach forward to the volley, thus promoting proper technique. Players should switch frequently so both can hit against the fence. This drill should be used for both forehands and backhands.

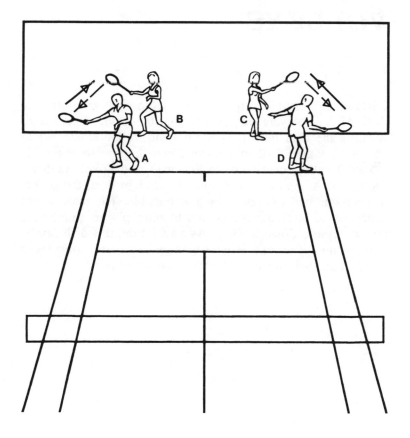

Volleys against the Fence

FIGURE EIGHT VOLLEYS

PLAYERS: 4

DRILL: This drill is similar to the figure eight groundstroke drill. All four players are positioned at the service line. Player A starts the drill by hitting a forehand volley crosscourt to Player C. Player C then volleys down the line to Player B. Player B volleys crosscourt to Player D, and D volleys down the line to A. As in the previous figure eight drill, the goal is to keep one ball in play as long as possible. The sequence of shots should be changed regularly to allow players to hit both crosscourt and down the line. As a variation, this drill can be done with large groups. Players who make an error must leave the drill and are substituted with a waiting player.

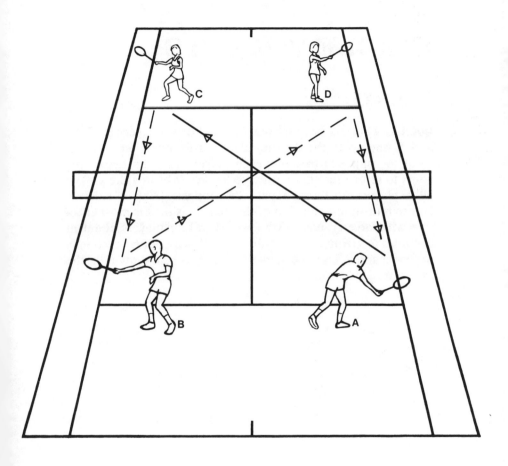

Figure Eight Volleys

CIRCLE VOLLEYS

PLAYERS: 4 or more

DRILL: This is a fast-moving, one-ball drill. Players B, C, D, and E line up in the doubles alley. As Player A feeds a ball from the opposite baseline, each player must run across the court to return the shot with a volley. After hitting the volley, each player must move past the opposite singles sideline before returning to the end of the line. This drill is most effective with large groups. With fewer than four players, the drill becomes too tiring. You can do this drill with either forehands or backhands. Use the cones for targets, as shown in the diagram.

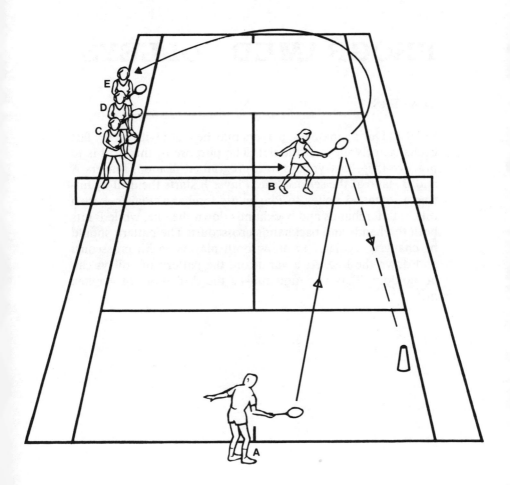

Circle Volleys

PROGRAMED VOLLEYS

PLAYERS: 2

DRILL: During matches, players may be faced with a very fast exchange of volleys at the net. The purpose of this drill is to practice these fast volleys in a programed fashion. Players A and B stand at the service line. Player B starts the drill by hitting a forehand volley to Player A's forehand. Player A then hits both forehands and backhands down the line, while B hits both forehands and backhands crosscourt. The pattern should be changed regularly to allow both players to hit crosscourt and down the line. As a variation, the pattern of volleys can be random. This variation makes the drill more of a reflex drill.

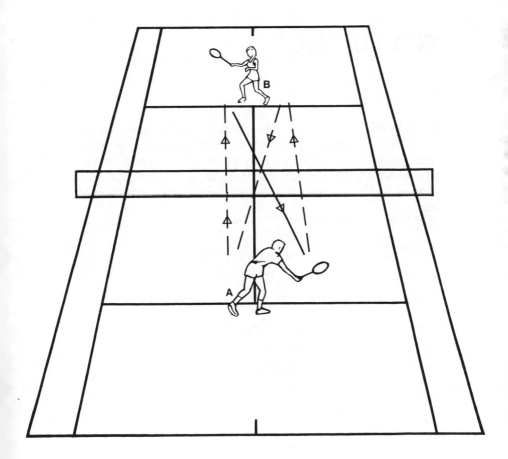

Programed Volleys

GO DRILL

PLAYERS: 2

DRILL: Both players A and B start at the service line. The drill begins with a volley, and as each player hits a volley, the player must move closer to the net. Players are forced to react quickly to each shot until it becomes impossible to make the shot. As soon as one player misses, the drill begins again at the service line.

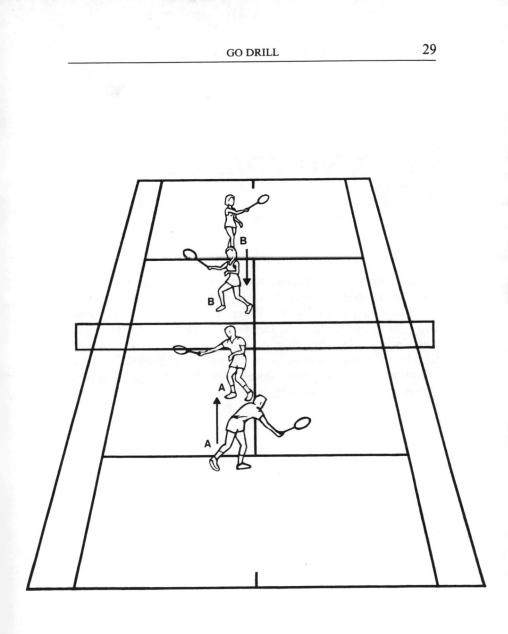

Go Drill

CLOSING VOLLEY DRILL

PLAYERS: 2 or 4

DRILL: This drill is similar to the go drill except one player stays at the baseline. Player A, standing at the baseline, starts the drill with a groundstroke. Player B starts at the service line and tries to move closer to the net after each volley. The drill starts again when one of the players misses. Players should take turns hitting volleys, both forehand and backhand. As a variation, the drill can be done in half of the court, which allows four players to use the same court.

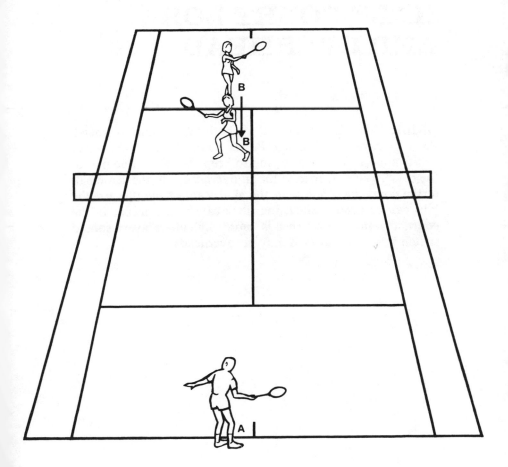

Closing Volley Drill

HALF-COURT LOB AND OVERHEAD

PLAYERS: 2 or 4

DRILL: This is a control drill for both the lob and overhead. Player A starts at the net and Player B is at the baseline. Player B hits a lob to Player A, trying to keep the lob in one half of the court. Player A tries to hit an overhead into the same half of the court. Depending on the skill level of the players, the lobs can be more challenging: they can be hit deeper in the court, making the overheads more difficult. Players should switch frequently so each may hit overheads.

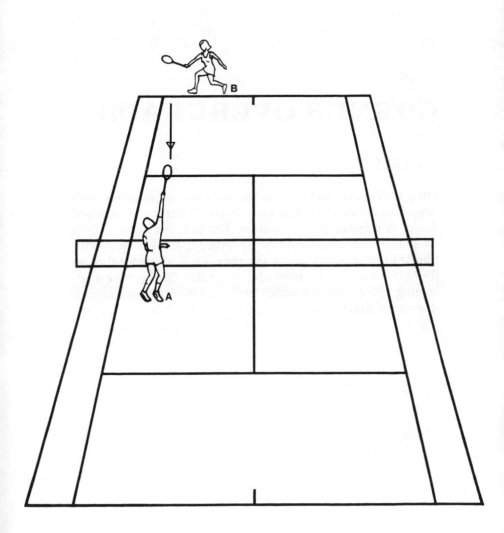

Half-court Lob and Overhead

CORNER OVERHEADS

PLAYERS: 2

DRILL: This is another control drill for the overhead and requires a number of tennis balls. Player B starts at the net and Player A remains at the baseline. The purpose of the drill is for Player B to alternate hitting overheads at the targets positioned in the corners. As in the previous drill, depending on the skill level of the players, the overheads can be more challenging. Players should switch frequently so each has a chance to practice overheads.

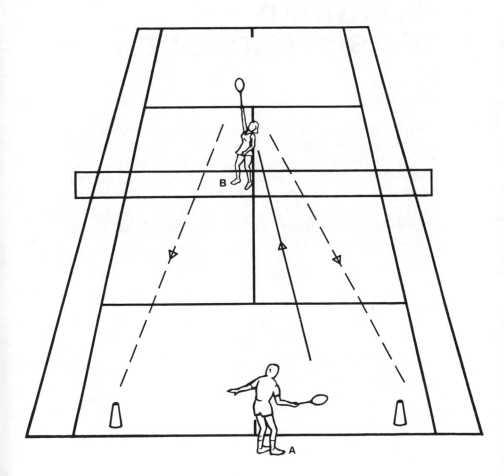

Corner Overheads

OVERHEAD CONSISTENCY DRILL

PLAYERS: 2

DRILL: The goal of this drill is to hit as many overheads as possible without a mistake. Player B starts at the net and Player A at the baseline. Player A hits backhand and forehand lobs to Player B, who must hit every overhead before the ball bounces. As soon as B makes a mistake, by either hitting the ball long, wide, or in the net, Player A comes to the net for overheads. As the players improve, the drill will last longer and become quite tiring.

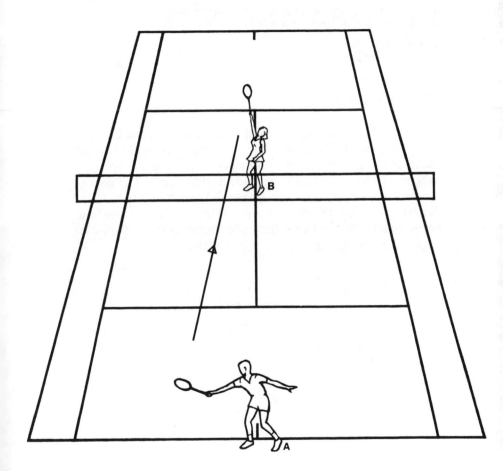

Overhead Consistency Drill

PROGRAMED NET DRILL

PLAYERS: 2 or 4

DRILL: This is another control and consistency drill using half of the court. Player B starts at the baseline and Player A starts at the net. Player B hits Player A a forehand volley, a backhand volley, and an overhead, in that order. The goal of the drill is to do this as long as possible with one ball. If the pattern is broken, the players should stop the ball in play and begin again. Players can switch after a set period of time or after the player at the net makes a mistake.

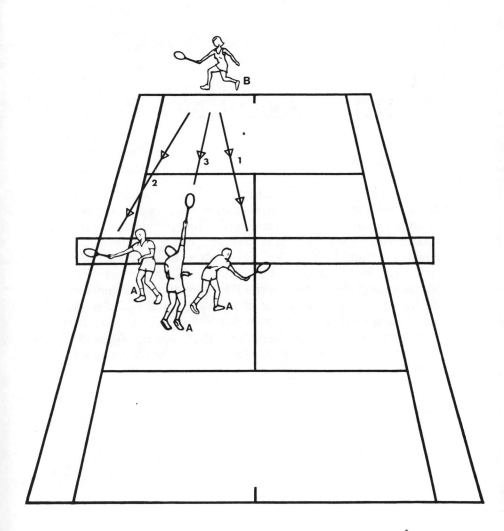

Programed Net Drill

TARGET SERVING

PLAYERS: 1 or more

DRILL: This is one of the easiest drills and also one of the most important for every player. Player A serves at a number of targets set up inside the service box. Inexperienced players should start with very large targets, and as a player develops, the targets should get smaller. The goals when serving should be: (1) get the ball in the service court, (2) hit the serve to different areas of the service court, (3) hit the serve with spin, (4) hit the serve with power. One of the biggest mistakes players make when serving is to try to serve with power too soon. In tennis, control is more important than power. Work to develop your control and technique first, and then think about power.

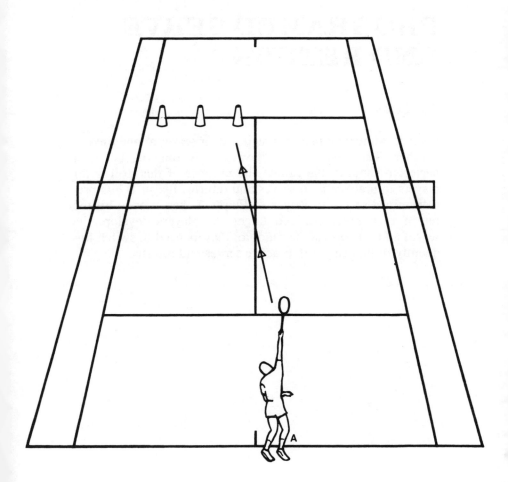

Target Serving

PROGRAMED SERVE AND RETURN

PLAYERS: 2

DRILL: Almost all players practice their serves at one time or another. The serve return, however, is one of the most neglected shots in the game. The purpose of this drill is for players to practice both serves and returns. Player B hits predetermined serves to Player A. Player A then tries to hit the return to a predetermined target. As players develop, the serves and returns can be random. Players need to switch frequently so that each can practice serves and returns.

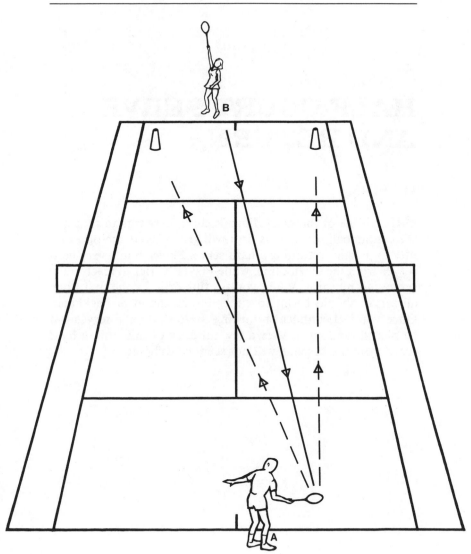

Programed Serve and Return

HALF-COURT SERVE AND RETURN

PLAYERS: 2

DRILL: One of the most difficult shots in tennis to return is the cannonball serve. This drill will give players the opportunity to practice returning a hard serve. Player B hits very hard serves from the service line, while Player A tries to react to the serve and return it. When you try this drill for the first time, all serves should be hit to either the forehand or backhand. Once you feel confident returning these shots, the serves can be placed randomly. After a few minutes of this drill, a hard serve from the baseline will not seem so difficult.

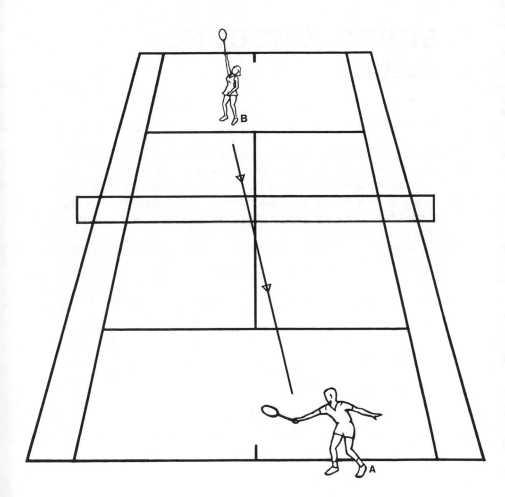

Half-court Serve and Return

SERVE, RETURN, RALLY

PLAYERS: 2

DRILL: Player B hits predetermined serves to Player A. Both players then rally the ball either crosscourt, as shown in the diagram, or down the line. The goal of each player should be to make each shot with good balance and technique. Serves should be hit to each half of the court, and the players should take turns serving.

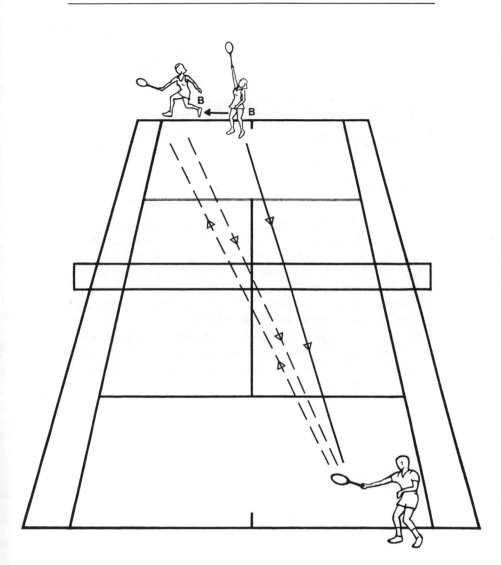

Serve, Return, Rally

SERVE, RETURN, VOLLEY

PLAYERS: 3 or 6

DRILL: This is a drill that allows players to practice every shot in a disciplined manner. Player A hits controlled serves to Player B. Player B must then hit a predetermined volley to Player C. Player C must hit the volley into one half of the court. There are many variations for this drill. Player B can hit a forehand volley and a backhand volley to Player C. Another variation would be for players B and C to rally the ball at random. In order to give all players a chance to hit each shot, players should rotate after a set period. Player A should go to the net to volley, C should move to hit serve returns, and B should change sides to serve.

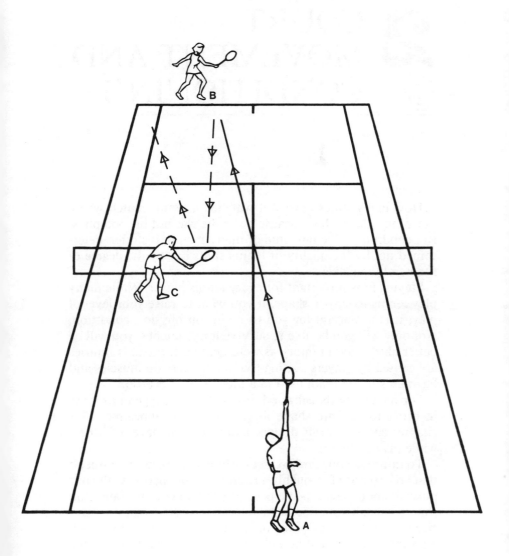

Serve, Return, Volley

2 COURT MOVEMENT AND CONDITIONING

How many times have you watched a tennis match where one of the players lost because he or she was not in good physical condition? The outcome of many matches is often determined not by the quality of tennis shots but by the degree of fitness of the players.

Staying fit is important for every tennis player. While many play tennis to stay in shape, if you want to raise your level of play, it is important for you to be in top physical condition. Not only will you be able to survive long matches, you will be better able to avoid injury as well. Quite a few tennis injuries are caused by players putting too much stress on muscles and ligaments that are not used to a high level of exertion.

For many, the thought of doing some other type of exercise in order to get into shape for tennis is not appealing. This chapter contains drills designed to raise your level of fitness while playing tennis.

To improve your cardiovascular fitness, experts recommend that you exercise for roughly a twenty-minute period with your pulse at about seventy-five percent of its maximum rate. You should consult your doctor to determine your maximum exercise pulse rate. Many of the drills in this chapter, if done with high intensity, should be able to raise your pulse rate to the desired rate.

There is some controversy among coaches about where in a practice session to insert physical conditioning drills. Some feel that conditioning drills should be done at the beginning of a practice session while players are fresh. Others feel that it should be near the end of a practice session so that players can give their all and maintain a high level of intensity for the entire session. You should work on these drills whenever it is convenient and will still prove beneficial. Tournament players will want to spend a good deal of time on these drills. Inexperienced players, however, will not need to devote as much practice time to these routines. They should concentrate more on the drills in the previous chapter.

LINE DRILL

PLAYERS: 1 or more

DRILL: One of the best ways to get into shape is running. More often than not, covering the court during a point requires a series of short, fast sprints. It makes sense for you to practice this type of running. Players start on one sideline and run back and forth across the court, touching each line as they go. If there are two or more courts together, the drill can be extended to include the lines on the other courts.

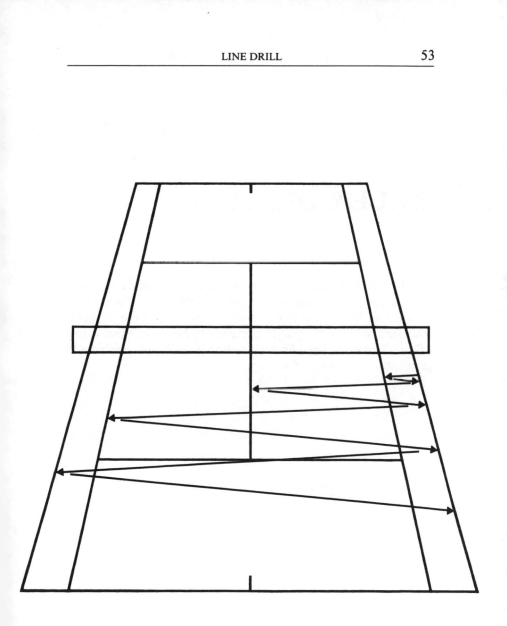

Line Drill

ALLEY DRILL

PLAYERS: 1 or more

DRILL: This is a shadow drill similar to shadowboxing drills. Players start at the baseline in the doubles alley. They move forward to the net, staying in the alley. Each time a player touches a sideline the player pretends to hit a forehand volley or a backhand volley. As each volley is "hit," players should concentrate on proper form.

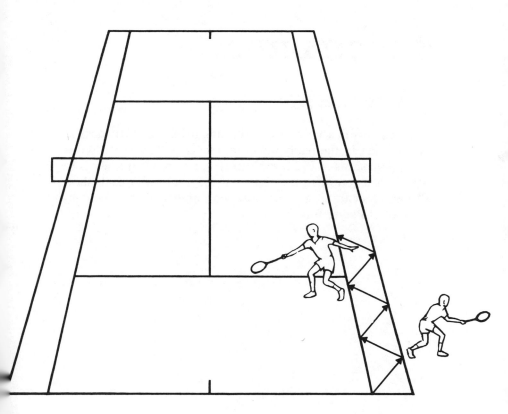

Alley Drill

TOUCH DRILL

PLAYERS: 2 or more

DRILL: This is a very simple running drill. Player B starts at the baseline in the ready position. Player A then hits a series of random shots to B. Player B must run to return the shots to A and then return to the center of the court after each shot. The players can hit a predetermined number of shots or continue until Player B is exhausted.

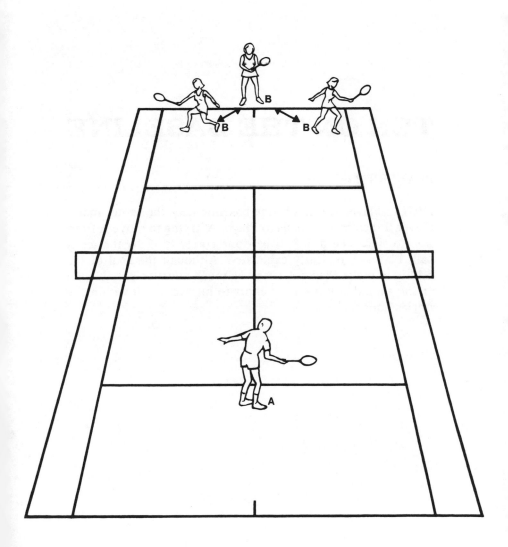

Touch Drill

TEN ON THE BASELINE

PLAYERS: 2 or more

DRILL: Player A starts at the baseline near the center mark. Player B then hits ten balls to Player A, trying to move A from side to side. The drill will be done correctly if, by the tenth ball, Player A is nearly exhausted. Although the goal of the drill is to make Player A cover as much court as possible, he or she should still make an effort to hit every ball within the singles boundaries.

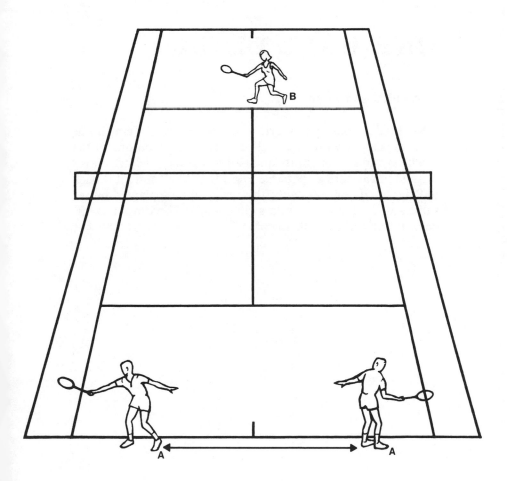

Ten on the Baseline

ONE-BALL DRILL

PLAYERS: 2 or more

DRILL: The goal of this drill is to make the players run as hard as possible to hit one ball. Player A starts on one of the sidelines and Player B hits one ball to the far sideline. Player A must run as hard as possible to get to the ball and hit it back to Player B. If done correctly, this drill will raise players' pulses substantially. Players should switch when it becomes too difficult to run for the ball.

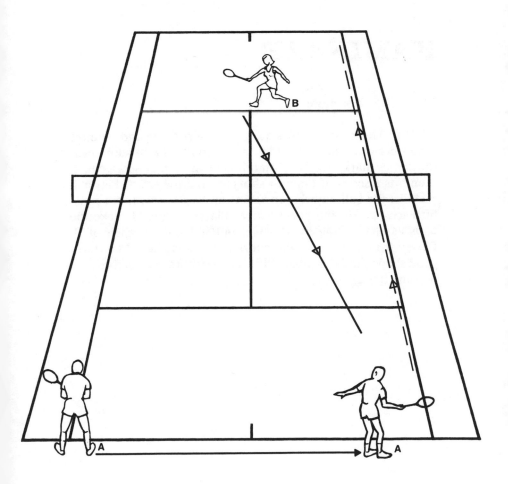

One-ball Drill

KAMIKAZE

PLAYERS: 2 or more

DRILL: This drill involves quite a bit of running and requires a number of tennis balls. Player B starts at the baseline near the center mark. Player A, standing at the center service line, then hits a series of random shots around the court. Player B may hit the ball anywhere within the singles court, but must hit each ball on the first bounce. Player A should make the balls as challenging as possible, but not out of reach of B. Player B must stay on the court until exhausted. Players in good shape should be able to hit sixty or more balls before they become tired.

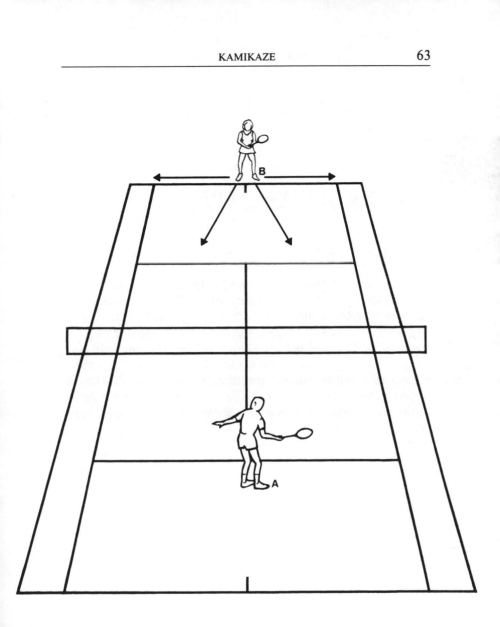

Kamikaze

OVER AND OUT

PLAYERS: 2 or more

DRILL: This is a two-ball drill and requires a number of tennis balls to carry out the entire sequence. Player B starts at the baseline near the center mark. Player A hits B two balls. The first ball is a forehand hit into the corner near the singles sideline. The second ball is a backhand hit into the opposite corner. As in the previous drills, A should make the balls as challenging as possible, but not out of reach of Player B. Players should concentrate on not moving back from the baseline to hit the second shot. The best players are able to hit both shots without retreating.

Over and Out

TWO-ON-ONE GROUNDSTROKES

PLAYERS: 3

DRILL: This is a very common drill, but it is also one of the best conditioning drills for tennis. Players A and B are positioned at the net. Player C starts at the baseline near the center mark. Players A and B must move C around the court, keeping the ball in play. It should be nearly impossible for Player C to hit the ball past A and B, and the object is to keep the ball in play for a long time. Players A and B should make the balls challenging for C but not out of reach. If Player C is in good shape, one ball should stay in play for quite a while.

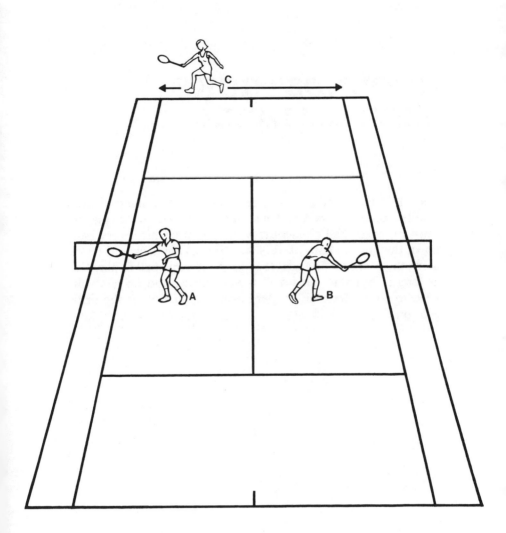

Two-on-one Groundstrokes

GROUNDSTROKE RHYTHM DRILL

PLAYERS: 2

DRILL: This is similar to the figure eight drill in the previous chapter. Both players A and B start at the baseline. One player must hit every ball crosscourt while the other hits every ball down the line, so both players will be moving back and forth along the baseline. The goal is to keep the same ball in play for as long as possible. This drill is very tiring, and players will need to concentrate on proper stroke production as the drill goes on.

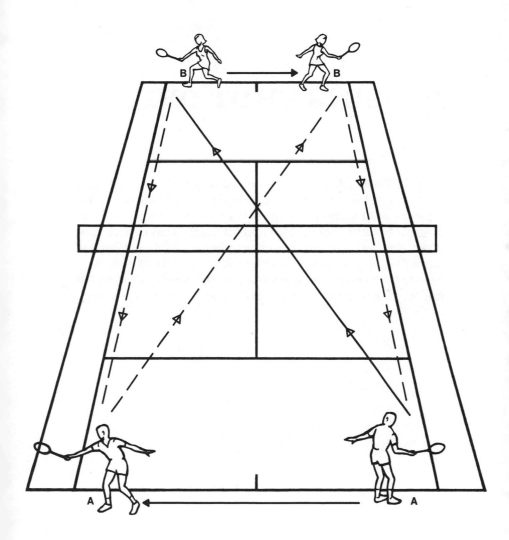

Groundstroke Rhythm Drill

PASSING SHOT DRILL

PLAYERS: 2

DRILL: Players A and B start on one half of the court, with A at the net and B at the baseline. The players rally the ball down the line until Player A hits one of his volleys crosscourt. Player B must then move crosscourt and hit a simulated passing shot down the line. For inexperienced players, A should hit the crosscourt volley after a predetermined number of hits. As a variation, A can move to try to cover the passing shot, and B can hit the ball crosscourt, down the line, or lob over A's head.

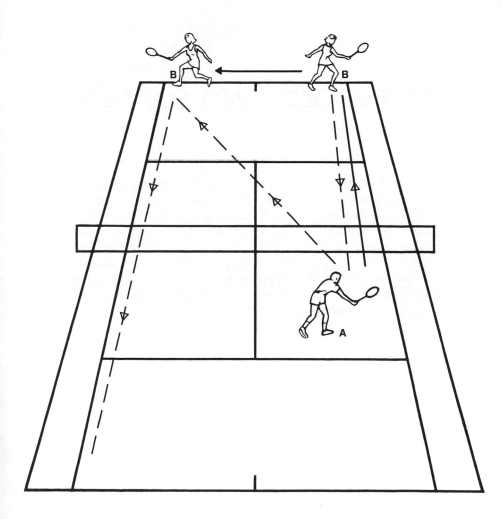

Passing Shot Drill

MODIFIED TWO-ON-ONE

PLAYERS: 2

DRILL: This drill is similar to the two-on-one groundstroke drill except this drill needs only two players. Both players start at the baseline, and the drill can begin with a serve or a groundstroke. After the ball is put into play, Player B stands in one part of the court, preferably one of the corners, and remains there. Player B then tries to move Player A around the court as much as possible, and A must return every ball to B. Player B must make Player A try hard for each shot, but should not hit the balls out of reach.

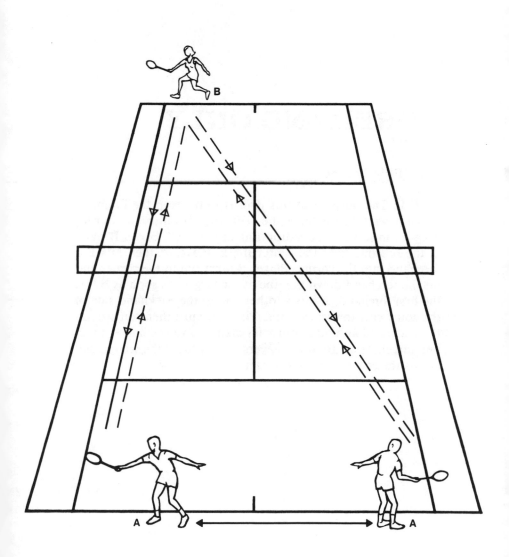

Modified Two-on-one

FOREHAND ONLY

PLAYERS: 2 or more

DRILL: The purpose of this drill is to develop the forehand into a powerful shot. Since the drill requires quite a bit of running it can serve as a conditioning drill as well. Player B starts at the baseline near the center mark. Player A then hits B a forehand into the corner. Player B must run to the corner and hit the forehand down the line at the target. As soon as B hits the first forehand, A hits another ball to the backhand side of the court near the service line. Player B must then run around the backhand and hit another forehand down the line at a second target. As a variation, players can try to hit the second ball across the court at the first target.

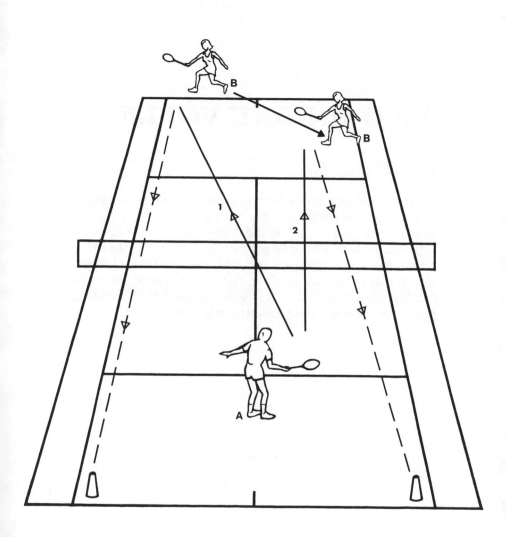

Forehand Only

TWO-ON-ONE VOLLEYS

PLAYERS: 3

DRILL: This drill is similar to the two-on-one groundstroke drill except one player is at the net hitting volleys. Players A and B at the baseline try to move the player at the net from side to side. It will be very difficult for Player C at the net to hit the ball past the players at the baseline, so the ball should stay in play for quite a while. If Player C is in good shape, the baseline players should mix in a few overheads. The players should switch when the volleyer is exhausted.

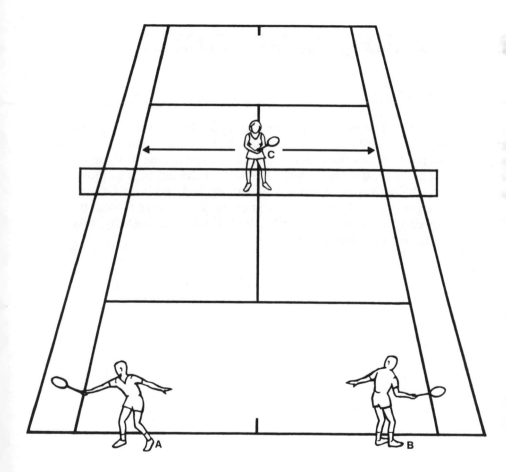

Two-on-one Volleys

HALF-COURT DRILL

PLAYERS: 2

DRILL: The purpose of this drill is for the players to try to move each other around using just half the court. Although the diagram shows the drill being done crosscourt, the drill can be done down-the-line as well. Player B at the net tries to move the baseline player around by hitting balls wide and short. Player A at the baseline tries to move the volleyer around by mixing in volleys and overheads. If done with intensity, this drill will be quite tiring.

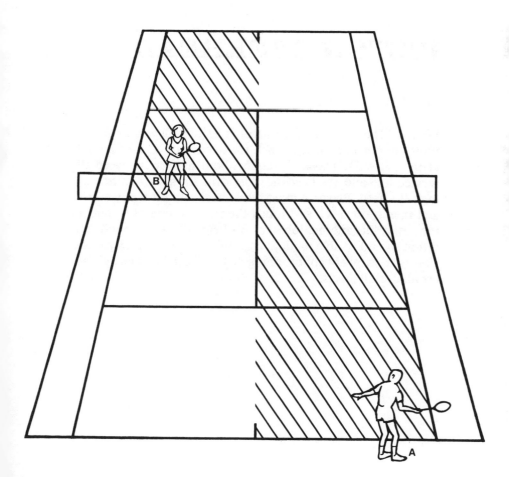

Half-court Drill

PISTON OVERHEAD

PLAYERS: 2 or more

DRILL: The purpose of this drill is to give players an opportunity to practice moving back for overheads. Player B starts at the net while Player A stands about halfway between the service line and the baseline. The drill starts as A hits a lob over B's head. Player B must move back and hit the overhead and then sprint back and touch the net. As soon as B touches the net, A hits another lob over B's head. Players in good condition should be able to hit at least twelve to fifteen overheads. This is an excellent conditioning drill and can be done by players at all skill levels.

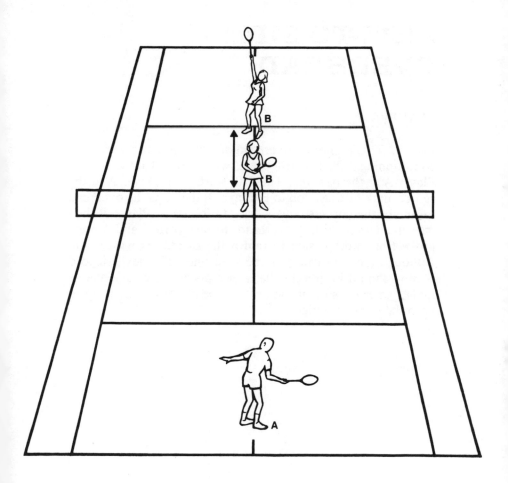

Piston Overhead

SIDE-TO-SIDE OVERHEAD

PLAYERS: 2

DRILL: This is another overhead drill that is also a very good conditioning drill. The drill begins with Player B at the net and Player A at the baseline. The drill starts with Player A at the center mark hitting a lob to B. Player B then hits the overhead to one of the corners, and A tries to lob back. Player B then tries to alternate hitting overheads to each corner, and A must move from side to side to return the overheads with a lob. Although the drill can be done with one ball, inexperienced players should keep a few balls in a pocket in case someone makes an error, so that the drill can be performed nonstop to keep the pulse rate high.

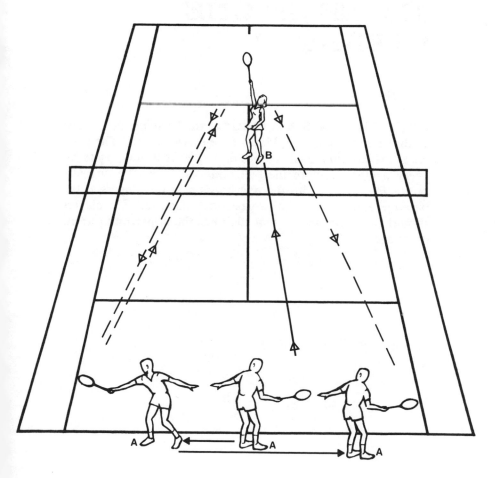

Side-to-side Overhead

THREE-ON-ONE OVERHEAD

PLAYERS: 4

DRILL: Players A, B, and C start at the baseline, positioned as shown in the diagram. Player D begins at the net. The players at the baseline must hit lobs only. Player B must try to hit every overhead before the ball bounces. It will be virtually impossible for D to hit the overheads past the players at the baseline, and D should quickly become exhausted. The players should switch around so that each has the opportunity to hit overheads.

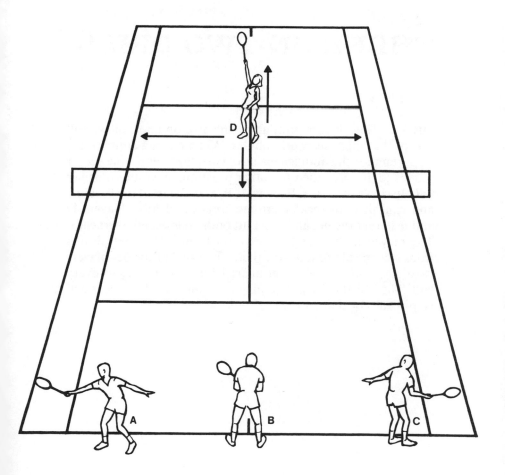

Three-on-one Overhead

THREE-ON-TWO DRILL

PLAYERS: 5

DRILL: This drill is similar to the two-on-one volley drill
except the emphasis is on doubles. When playing doubles it is
important for the doubles team to work together. If one player
moves to the side, then the other must move with him or her
to help cover the court. Players A, B, and C start at the baseline
and can hit both regular groundstrokes and lobs. Players D
and E start at the net and must hit both volleys and overheads.
The players at the baseline must try to move the net players
from side to side or lob over them. The goal of the net players
is to stay about twelve feet apart while still getting to every
ball. The ball should stay in play for quite a while since it will
be difficult for the net players to hit winners.

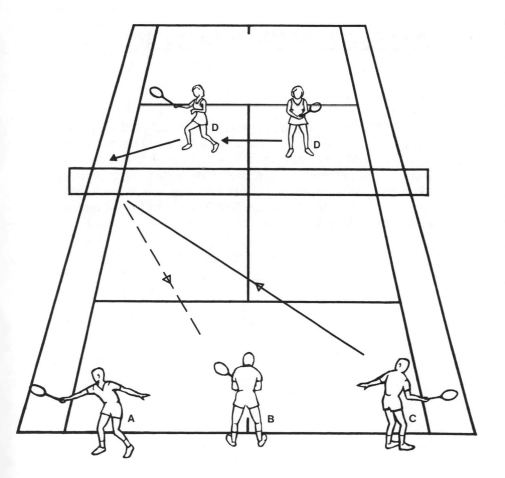

Three-on-two Drill

AUSSIE SCRAMBLE

PLAYERS: 2 or more

DRILL: This is one of the toughest conditioning drills for tennis. Even the most highly conditioned athlete will have trouble doing this drill for more than two minutes. Both players A and B start at the net, and A is essentially the feeder. Player A tries to make B scramble at the net by hitting soft shots from side to side. Player B must let each ball bounce and must return each shot back to A.

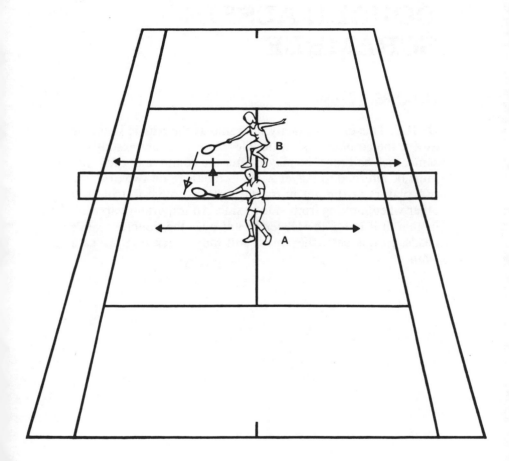

Aussie Scramble

DOUBLE AUSSIE SCRAMBLE

PLAYERS: 3 or more

DRILL: This drill is exactly the same as the Aussie scramble except the emphasis is on doubles. The rules are exactly the same, each ball must be played after the bounce and each shot must be returned to Player A. As in the three-on-two drill, the two players at the net must stay within twelve feet of each other when moving from side to side. An important variation in this drill is for the feeder to lob over the doubles team's heads. In this case, they must still move back together as a team.

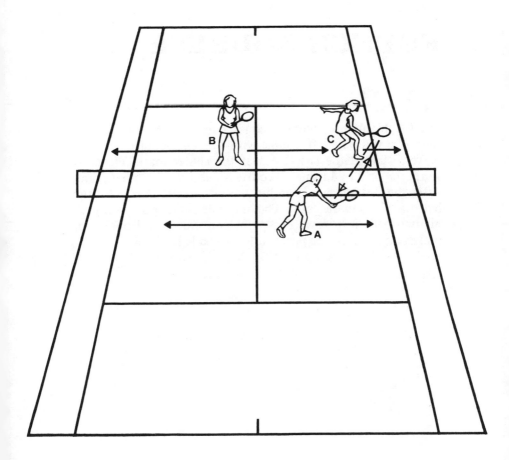

Double Aussie Scramble

FRENCH DOUBLES

PLAYERS: 4

DRILL: If you have ever played table tennis with four players, then you will have no trouble with French Doubles. All four players start at the baseline near the center mark. Player A starts the drill by hitting a "courtesy" shot to the other team. After the first ball has been hit, the players are free to hit the ball anywhere in the court. The only rule is that no player may hit two balls in a row. The point continues until one team makes an error or one player hits two balls in a row.

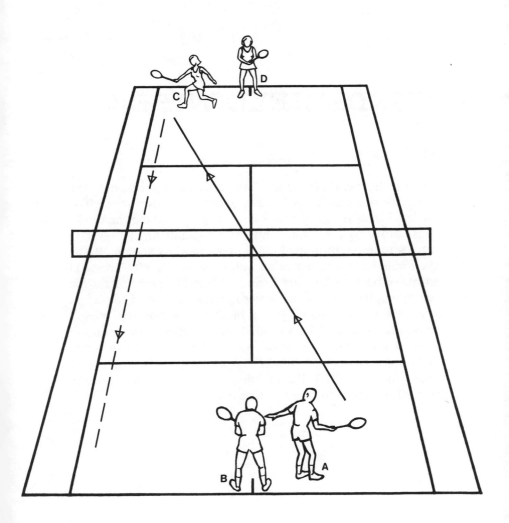

French Doubles

WINDSHIELD WIPER

PLAYERS: 2 or more

DRILL: In this drill, Player B starts at the baseline near the center mark while Player D starts near the singles sideline. The feeder, Player A, hits a ball wide to B's right so that he or she must move to hit a forehand. At the same time, Player D moves to the right toward the center mark. As soon as B hits the forehand, the feeder hits a ball wide to D's left, forcing D to move back to hit a backhand. While D moves to hit the backhand, B returns to the center mark, and so on. The players should move in tandem, giving them the "windshield wiper" look. Players C and E, behind B and D, should move in the same manner and hit shadow strokes. The players can rotate after a predetermined number of shots, or they can switch when they are tired. Players should try to hit all the balls toward the cones to avoid hitting the feeder.

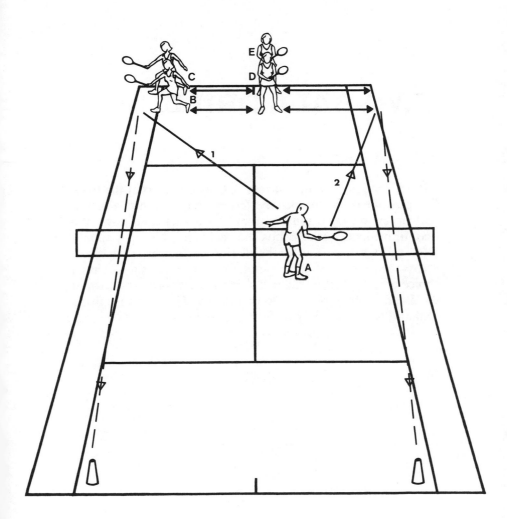

Windshield Wiper

TWO-BALL DRILL

PLAYERS: 2 or more

DRILL: In this drill, the players B, C, and D start at the baseline near the center mark. The feeder, Player A, hits a ball in the corner so that B must run and hit a backhand down the line. Immediately after B hits the backhand, Player A should hit a short ball to the forehand side so that B must sprint across the court to make the shot. On the second shot, B has a choice of either hitting the ball sharply crosscourt, as shown in the diagram, or pushing it down the line. This is a very tiring drill and is best done with a group of players.

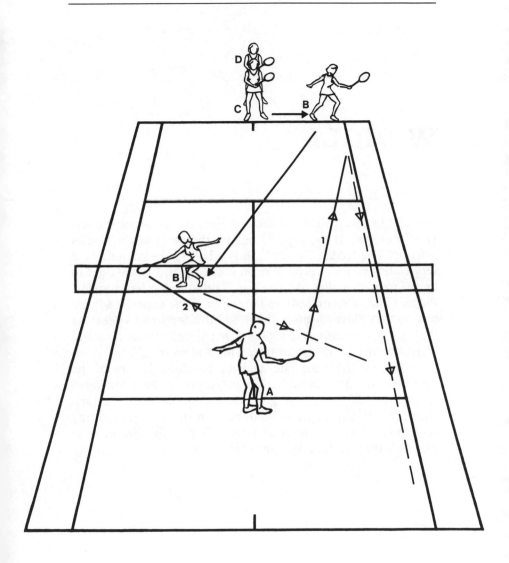

Two-ball Drill

W DRILL

PLAYERS: 3 or more

DRILL: In this drill, there are two lines of players at the service line—one at the center line and the other at the singles sideline. The feeder, Player G, hits a ball to the center of the service box so that Player B must move up and to the right to hit a forehand volley. As soon as B hits the forehand volley, Player G hits a second ball to the center of the opposite service box so that Player A must move to hit a forehand volley. As Player A is moving out to hit his or her volley, Player B should be recovering to the center line. The players should try to hit their volleys down the line, and the resulting pattern of the balls gives the drill its name. The players move back and forth to hit two volleys and then go to the end of the line. As a variation, the W drill can also be done with the volleyers hitting backhands. Use the cones as targets. This will reinforce the idea of hitting volleys deep into the court.

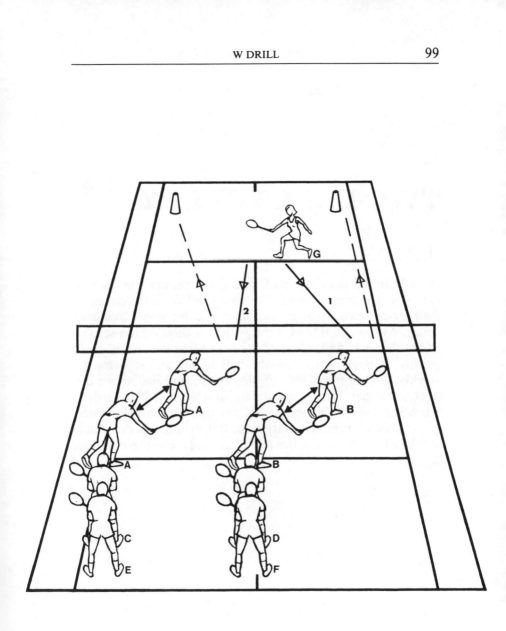

W Drill

TWO-BALL VOLLEY

PLAYERS: 2 or more

DRILL: In this drill, players B and C start at the T of the service line. The feeder, Player A, hits a low ball to the center of the service box so that B must move to hit a low forehand volley. As soon as B has hit the volley, A should hit a second ball to the backhand side near the net so that B must move as quickly as possible to play the ball in the air. If B moves quickly enough and is able to play the second ball above the level of the net, then B can try to hit a winner. If the ball is below the level of the net, B must try to push the volley back deep into the court. As a variation, this drill can begin with a backhand volley. As in the previous drills, use the cones as targets.

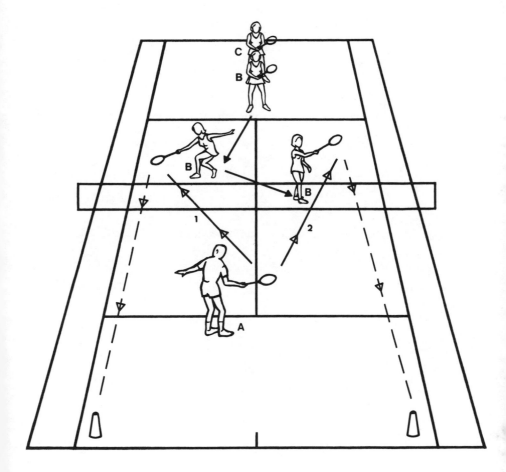

Two-ball Volley

3 GAME SITUATIONS

How many matches have you played where you lost a crucial point because you hit the ball down the line when you should have gone crosscourt? If you are like most tennis players, this has probably happened to you at one time or another. The reason some tennis players make the same strategic mistakes repeatedly is that they don't practice hitting the proper shot at the proper time.

Tennis players need to understand that certain strategic situations occur frequently in tennis matches. If you have ever watched a professional tennis match, you have probably seen players following a shot to the net and then hitting the volley to the open court. They can hit the winning volley consistently because they have practiced the same shot over and over.

Tennis is a game involving instant reactions. It is important that you rehearse common situations, so that when they occur in a match you will be able to react properly in that instant. The drills in this chapter will help you practice the game situations that occur frequently, so that on the next crucial point in a match you will immediately know what to do.

While these drills will benefit all players, they will be most important for the intermediate to advanced player. Players at this level will want to set aside a good portion of practice time for these drills. Many players will want to devote as much as half their practice session to match situation drills. By rehearsing the common situations in practice, you can develop the shots you need to win matches.

MINI-TENNIS

PLAYERS: 2 or 4

DRILL: Many points are lost at the net because the players do not have the "feel" of hitting touch shots. This drill allows players to practice hitting touch shots near the net. Players A and B start at the service line and play points using only the area formed by both service boxes. Each point begins with a groundstroke, and the first shot must be a "courtesy" shot. The only other rule is that the players may not hit volleys. The players should take turns starting each point in order to eliminate any advantage from hitting the first shot. Players are free to keep score or just play points.

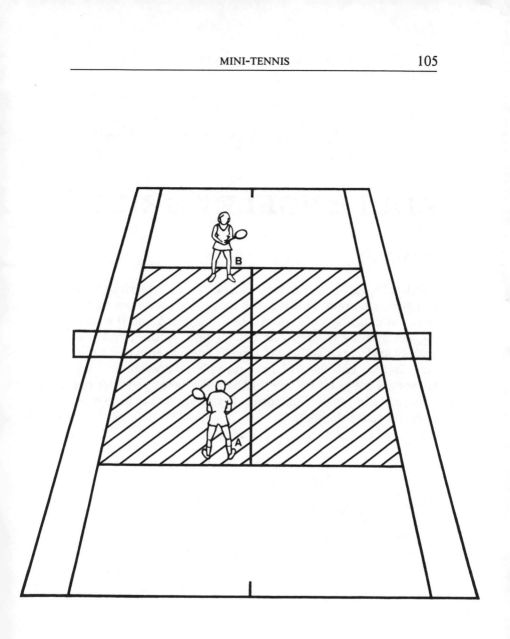

Mini-Tennis

ANGLE VOLLEY DRILL

PLAYERS: 2

DRILL: Sharply angled volleys can be particularly tricky shots in a game situation. This is a drill that affords players a chance to practice hitting such volleys. Both players A and B start at the net and try to keep one ball in play, hitting volleys as sharply angled as possible. As soon as one player makes a mistake, another ball should be put into play. Although the players should try to hit volleys, the ball may be played after one bounce. As in the previous drill, players are free to keep score or just practice the shots.

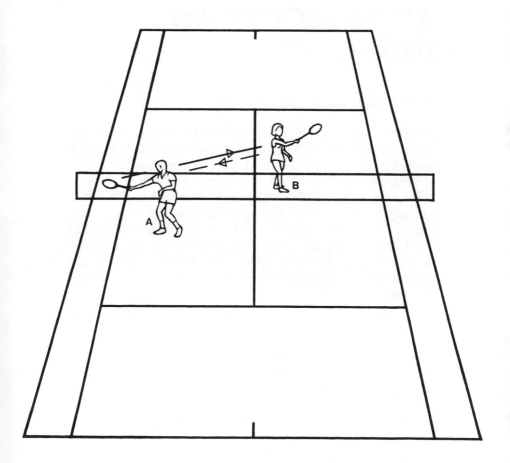

Angle Volley Drill

APPROACH SHOT DRILL

PLAYERS: 2 or more

DRILL: This is a three-ball drill with emphasis on the approach shot. Player B begins at the baseline near the center mark. Player A, the feeder, is at the opposite baseline. Player A hits the first ball into the corner so that Player B must move to hit a backhand return. Following that shot, A hits B a shot near the service line so that B must move in to hit a forehand approach shot. B continues to move to the net and A finishes the drill by hitting B a volley. This drill should also be done starting with a forehand. Since the emphasis is on the approach shot, if B misses the approach shot, the volley should be omitted.

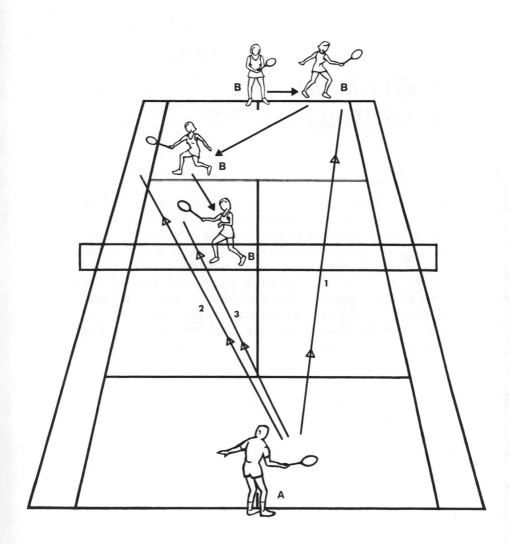

Approach Shot Drill

TWO-PERSON PASSING SHOT

PLAYERS: 2

DRILL: This drill simulates one of the most common situations in tennis. Namely, one player comes to the net, and his or her opponent attempts to pass the player at the net. Player A starts the drill by hitting a volley to Player B, who is positioned at the T of the service line. Player B must hit each volley down the line and then move into the net. Player A then tries to pass B down the line, crosscourt, or lob over B's head. If the ball is still in play after the first three shots, then the players should play out the point. The players are free to keep score or just practice.

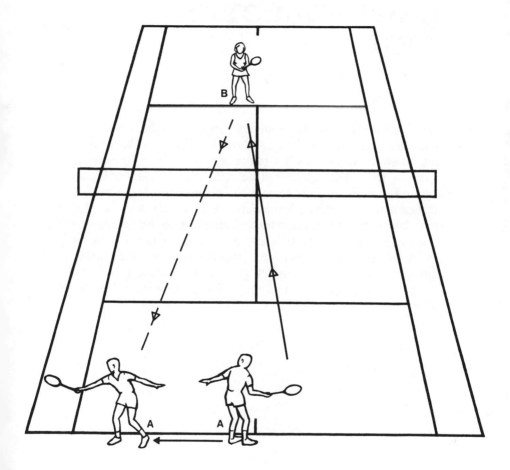

Two-person Passing Shot

SHOT SELECTION DRILL

PLAYERS: 2

DRILL: Player B stands about eight feet inside the service line near the center line and hits a shot at random to Player A at the baseline. As soon as B hits the shot to A, B has the choice to move to the left, right, or close in on the net. Depending on where B moves, A must choose the proper shot to try to pass B. For example, Player A may choose to hit a sharply angled crosscourt shot. If Player B moves too close to the net, A may want to lob over B's head. These are just some of the possible shots Player A could choose. This decision must be made quickly, thus simulating match play. After the first two shots, the players may play out the point. The players should switch after every four or five points.

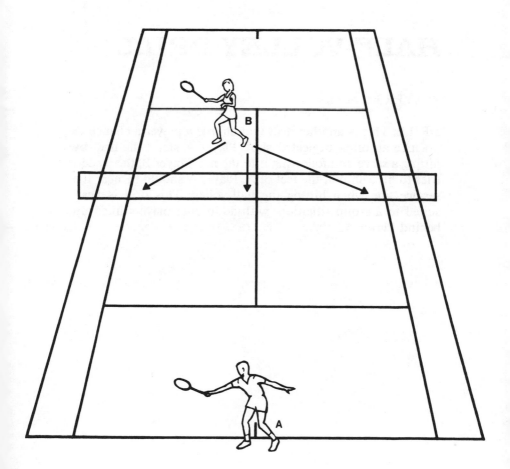

Shot Selection Drill

HALF-VOLLEY DRILL

PLAYERS: 2 or more

DRILL: This is another drill that affords a player a chance to practice an often neglected shot. Player A starts the drill by hitting a serve and following it to the net. Player B, the feeder, tries to hit a shot at the feet of A. Player A should be near the service line when hitting the half-volley. This drill is best-suited to a group situation, with additional players lined up behind Player A.

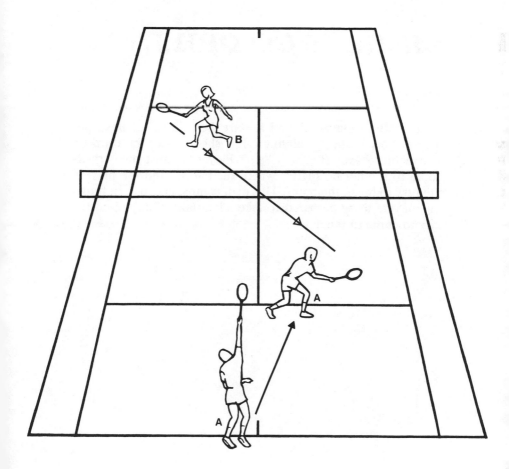

Half-volley Drill

SINGLES GO DRILL

PLAYERS: 2

DRILL: Both players A and B start the drill at the baseline. The players begin by rallying a few shots. After the third or fourth hit, Player B shouts "go." Player A must then try to come to the net no matter where the ball is, and the players then try to finish the point. This drill is most effective in training players to be prepared to take advantage of any opportunity to come to the net.

Singles Go Drill

SINGLES MUST ATTACK

PLAYERS: 2

DRILL: Both players A and B begin the drill at the baseline, rallying. As soon as one player hits the ball inside the opponent's service line, the opponent must come to the net and the players try to play out the point. It is possible that both players could be at the net at the same time. The goal for the players is to keep the ball deep in their opponent's court so that their opponent will never have a chance to come to the net.

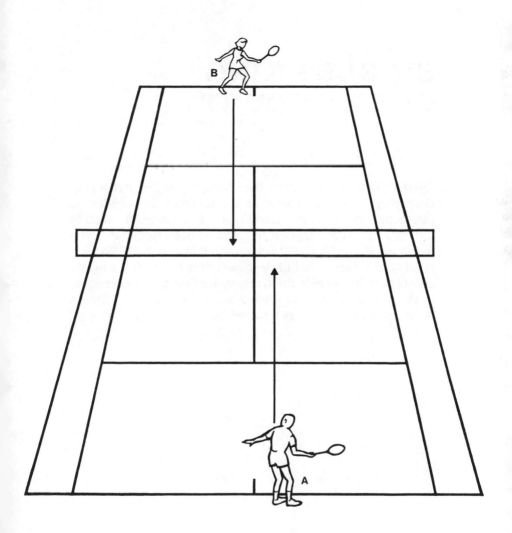

Singles Must Attack

SINGLES KING OF THE COURT

PLAYERS: 3 or more

DRILL: This drill simulates the variety of singles match play. Both players A and B start at the baseline. The feeder, an instructor or other player standing outside the court, starts by hitting a ball to B. Player B hits an approach shot and moves to the net. Player A then tries to pass B at the net. If Player A is successful, then A is still the King of the Court. If B wins the point, then B becomes the King of the Court, and A must go to the end of the line. If A wins five points in a row, then A must retire as king and is replaced by another player.

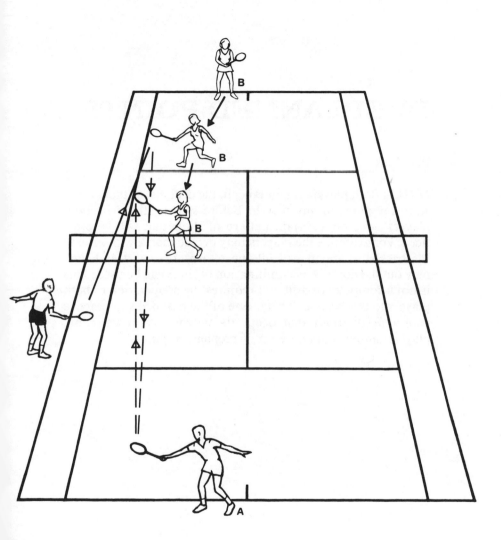

Singles King of the Court

PREPLANNED POINTS

PLAYERS: 2

DRILL: Both players A and B begin the drill just as they would start any point in any match. Before starting the drill, both players agree on a certain pattern of shots that will be practiced. For example, the players may decide that A will serve to B's backhand and B will hit the return crosscourt and then play out the point. Any combination of shots can be used. This is not a competitive drill and requires the cooperation of both players to be effective. This is one of the best drills to practice common situations that occur in matches. As a variation, players can play an entire set of preplanned points.

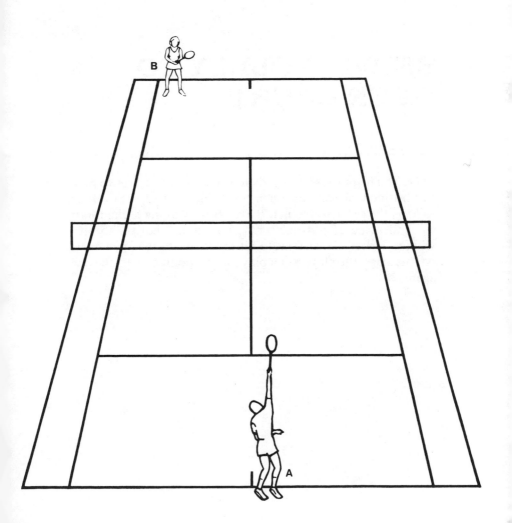

Preplanned Points

SERVE, VOLLEY TO OPEN COURT

PLAYERS: 2 or more

DRILL: The purpose of this drill is to allow the server to practice hitting volleys to the open court. Player A serves to B and follows the serve to the net. Player B tries to make the return as challenging as possible for A, but should not try to hit a winner. Player A then tries to hit the volley to the open court. At this stage, the players can play out the point or start the drill again.

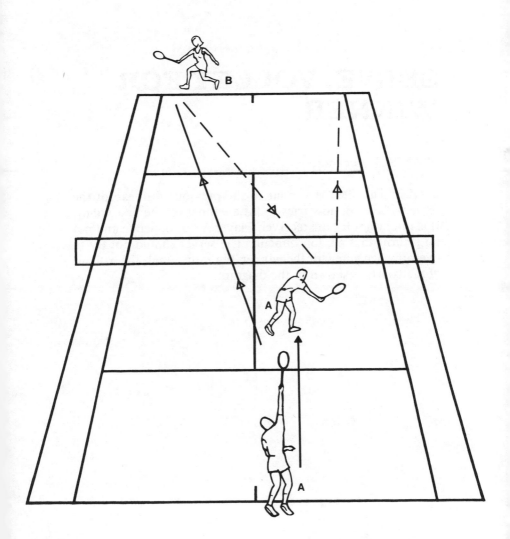

Serve, Volley to Open Court

SERVE, VOLLEY FOR WINNER

PLAYERS: 2 or more

DRILL: This drill is similar to the previous drill except the server, Player B, now tries to hit a winner off the first volley. It is important for the receiver, Player A, to cooperate and not hit returns that are too difficult. The server should not try to overhit when going for the winner, but rather angle the ball out of the court, as shown in the diagram.

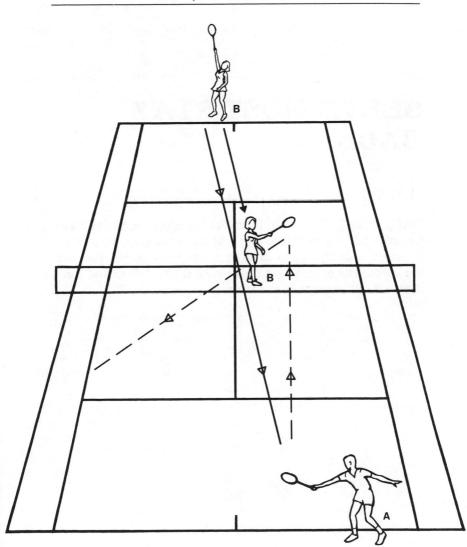

Serve, Volley for Winner

SERVE MUST STAY BACK

PLAYERS: 2

DRILL: The purpose of this drill is to practice groundstrokes in a competitive situation. Player B starts the point by serving to player A. Both players must then stay back as they play out the point. The emphasis is on keeping the ball deep and forcing your opponent to make an error.

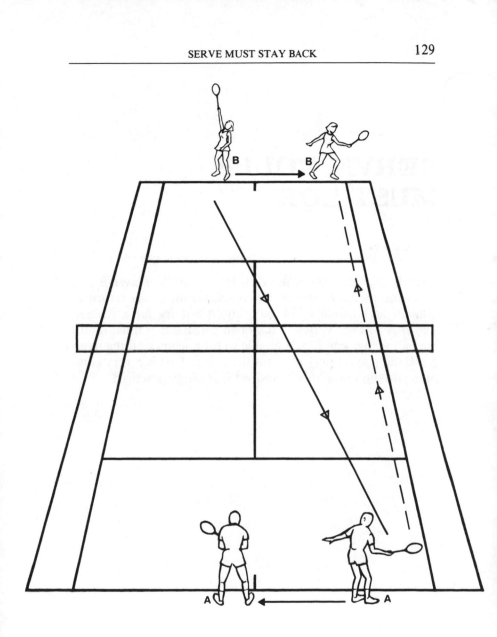

Serve Must Stay Back

SERVE, VOLLEY MUST LOB

PLAYERS: 2

DRILL: Player A starts the drill by serving to Player B and following the serve to the net. B should make the return as difficult as possible for A but should not try for a winner. Player A hits the volley to the open court and B must return the ball with a lob. If A is unable to hit a winner off the overhead, the players may play out the point. This is a very common situation in matches, and yet it is rarely practiced.

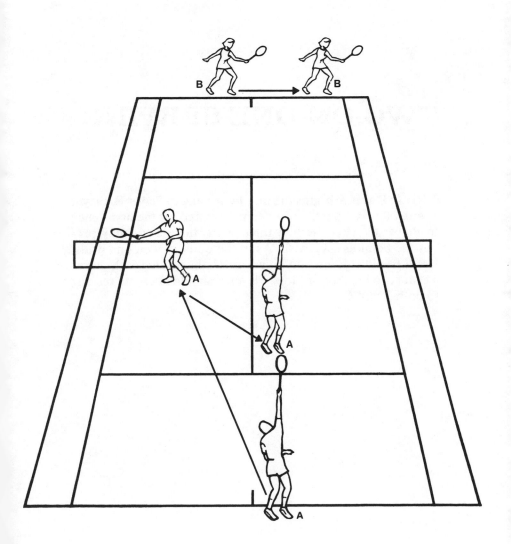

Serve, Volley Must Lob

TWO-ON-ONE SERVING

PLAYERS: 3

DRILL: Player A begins the drill by serving to Player B. Player A must then follow the serve to the net and hit the first volley to Player C. After the first three shots, the players may play out the point as they wish. As in the other two-on-one drills, it will be difficult for A to hit a winner, thus giving each player a chance to hit a lot of shots. Player A should alternate serving to both B and C.

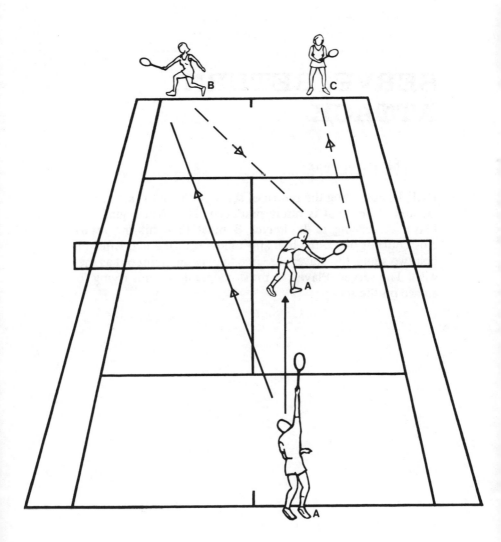

Two-on-one Serving

SERVE, RETURN, ATTACK

PLAYERS: 2 or more

DRILL: Following the return of serve to the net is a common tactic, but one that is rarely practiced. This drill begins with Player A serving to B. Player B must then hit the return crosscourt or down the line and follow it to the net. After the first two shots, the players are free to play the point out as they wish. The server, Player A, must cooperate by not trying for an ace on the serve.

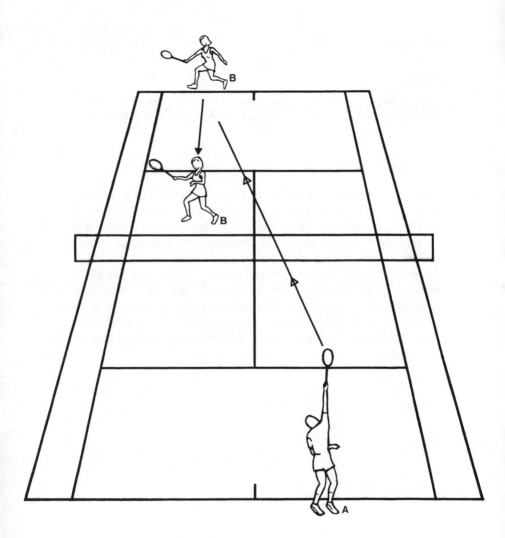

Serve, Return, Attack

SECOND SERVE DRILL

PLAYERS: 2

DRILL: This drill is designed to help players develop the concentration and consistency necessary to get their second serve in during a pressured game situation. Player A starts the point by serving to B. However, Player A has only one serve in this drill and thus should treat the ball as a "second serve." If A misses the serve, it is considered a double fault and the point is awarded to Player B. Since A has only one serve, this is an excellent drill to practice one's second serve in a competitive situation. After the serve, the players are free to play out the point as they wish. Players should switch after serving four or five points.

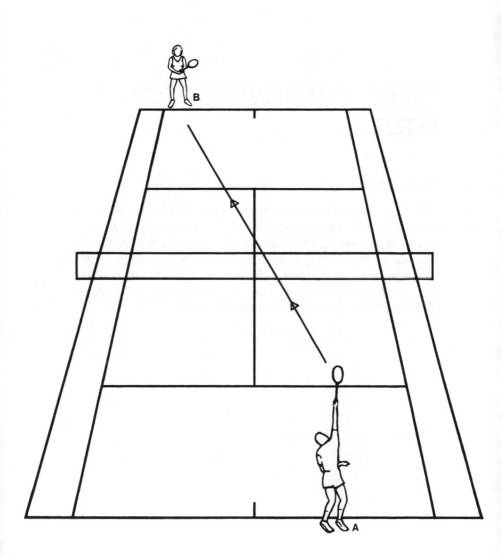

Second Serve Drill

SERVE PROTECTION DRILL

PLAYERS: 2

DRILL: This drill reinforces the concept of winning your own serve. The drill begins with Player B serving to A. After the serve, the players play the point as they would a regular match. As long as Player B is able to win the serving games, B will continue to serve. As soon as B loses a serving game to A, the serve switches to Player A. The players can play an entire set in this manner or just play a series of games.

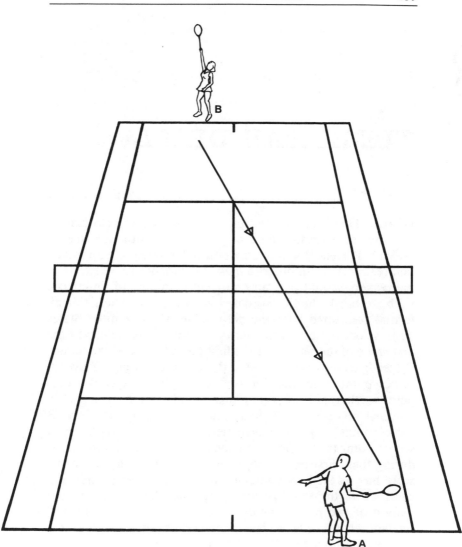

Serve Protection Drill

TIE-BREAK DRILL

PLAYERS: 2

DRILL: This is another simple drill designed to help players develop concentration for a pressured game situation: the tie breaker. Players B and A play points following the approved tie-break format. In order to make the practice more effective, the players should play an entire set or match of tie breaks. Each tie break should be scored as one game. The tie-break format (reprinted with the permission of the United States Tennis Association) is as follows: Player A, having served the first game of the set, serves the first point from the right court; Player B serves points two and three (left and right); Player A serves points four and five (left and right); Player B serves point six (left) and, after they change ends, point seven (right); Player A serves points eight and nine (left and right); Player B serves points ten and eleven (left and right); and Player A serves point twelve (left). A player who reaches seven points during these first twelve points wins the game and set. If the score has reached six points all, the players change ends and continue in the same pattern until one player establishes a margin of two points, which gives him or her the game and set. Note that the players change ends every six points and that the player who serves the last point of one of these six point segments also serves the first point of the next one (from right court).

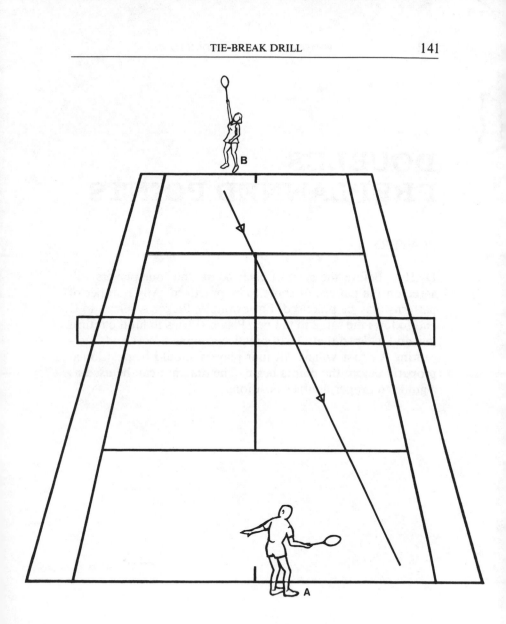

Tie-break Drill

DOUBLES PREPLANNED POINTS

PLAYERS: 4

DRILL: Before the start of each point, the four players will agree on the pattern of shots to be practiced. Any number of patterns may be practiced. For example, Player A serves to C and follows the serve to the net. Player C tries to hit the return low and wide so that D can practice moving across and intercepting A's first volley. All four players should be positioned properly before the points begin. The diagram can be used as a guide to proper doubles positions.

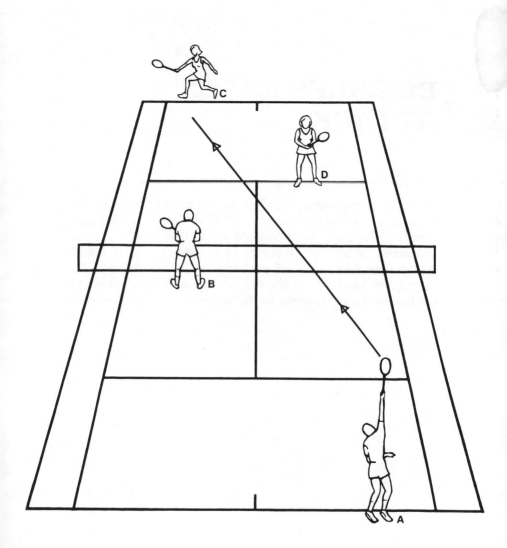

Doubles Preplanned Points

DOUBLES MUST ATTACK

PLAYERS: 4

DRILL: All four players begin at the baseline hitting groundstrokes. As soon as someone hits a ball inside his or her opponents' service line, the opponents must move into the net. It
is possible for all four players to be at the net at once, which
would allow for some quick exchanges at the net. The goal for
the players is to keep the ball deep so that their opponents will
not have a chance to come to the net.

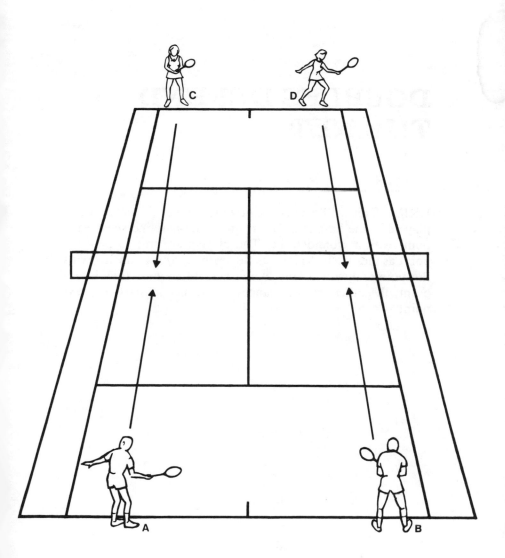

Doubles Must Attack

DOUBLES DEFEND THE NET

PLAYERS: 4

DRILL: This drill begins with two players at the net and two players at the baseline. The team at the baseline starts each point with a groundstroke. The players are free to play the point as they wish. As long as the team starting at the net wins the points, they will stay at the net. As soon as they lose a point, the other team advances to the net to start the next point.

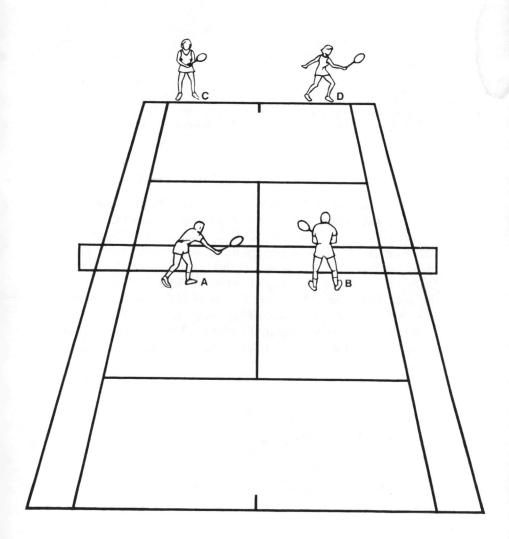

Doubles Defend the Net

HOT SEAT DRILL

PLAYERS: 4

DRILL: This drill is designed so that Player B, the player in the "hot seat," can practice returning a shot hit directly at him or her. Player C starts the drill by serving to Player A. Although A would normally try to hit the return crosscourt, for the purpose of the drill A hits the ball to Player D. Player D then hits the volley directly at Player B. Player B must reflex the ball back, and the players can then play out the point. Depending on the skill level of the players, D can make the volley to B as challenging as D wishes. The players should change frequently so every player has a chance in the hot seat.

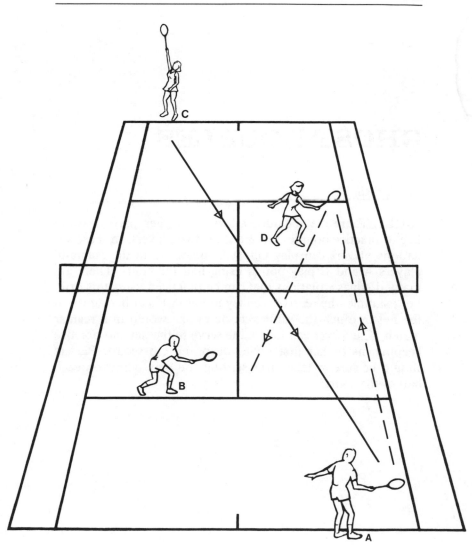

Hot Seat Drill

GHOST DOUBLES

PLAYERS: 2

DRILL: There may be quite a few times when players would like to practice doubles but are short two players. In these situations players can play Ghost Doubles. As in the diagram, players A and B play points using half the court. There are many doubles situations that can be practiced using this drill. For example, the receiver can try to follow his or her return to the net in much the same way he or she would in a regular match. The server can follow the serve to the net and practice keeping his or her first volley deep and crosscourt. Players should be sure to take turns serving and play points on each half of the court.

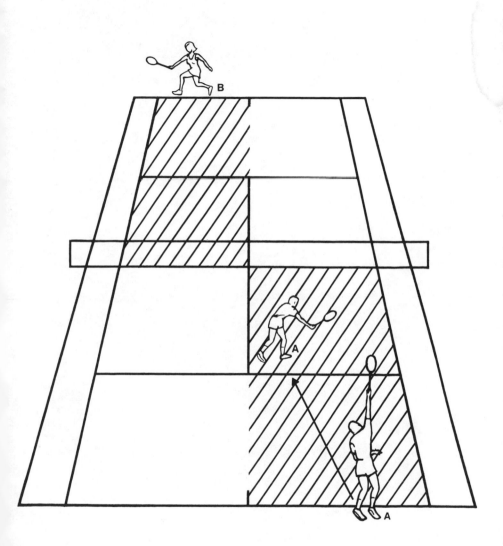

Ghost Doubles

4 PRACTICE GAMES

At some point, tennis may become boring for you. This is natural and happens to the best players in the world. What can you do, besides putting your racket in the closet, to regain a fresh attitude toward tennis? One answer would be to include some games in your practice session.

Livening up your practice session with games will help eliminate the monotony of hitting countless numbers of tennis balls over the net and will help restore your enthusiasm for the sport. Just about every drill in this book can be made into some type of a game. For most players, adding competition to a drill will be just the thing to relieve the monotony of practice. The three games shown here are but a few examples of the many ways you can spice up a dull practice.

AROUND THE WORLD

PLAYERS: any number

DRILL: Around the World is one of the most popular group games in tennis for both adults and juniors. The drill starts with two lines of players at opposing baselines near the center. marks. Player A starts the point with a groundstroke to Player D, and then exits to the right and runs to the end of the line on the opposite side. Player D returns the shot to Player B, and exits to the right and runs to the end of the line on the opposite side. Each player continues this, trying to keep the ball in play inside the singles court. As soon as someone misses, they are out and must leave the game. The only rule is that volleys are not allowed. When all but two of the players have been eliminated, the two play the best of three points to determine the champion of Around the World. Since they cannot possibly run to the other side of the court after each shot, they must spin around in a circle after they hit.

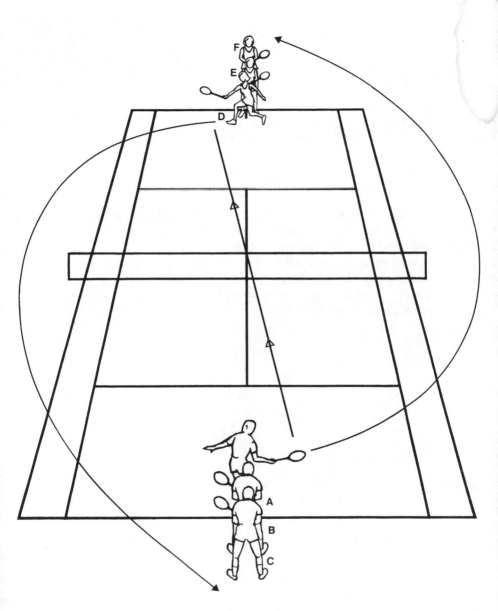

Around the World

TWENTY-ONE

PLAYERS: 2

DRILL: This is simply a game of points played without a serve. Each point is started with a "courtesy" groundstroke and "ping pong" scoring is used. The scoring system used makes each point equally important and makes each game interesting. The first player to reach twenty-one points is the winner. A game may be won by a margin of one or two points at the discretion of the players.

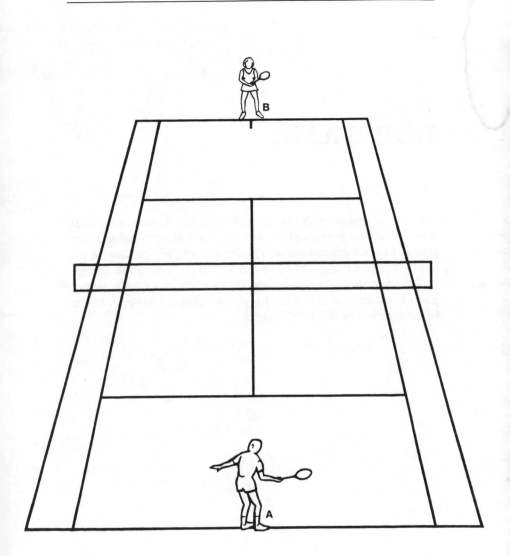

Twenty-one

LOB GAME

PLAYERS: 6

DRILL: The players should be positioned as shown in the diagram. The four players at the baseline can hit only lobs. Their goal is to lob over the players at the net so they cannot hit an overhead. The players at the net may not go behind the service line to hit a shot. Points are won and lost as in a regular game. Each team should rotate its players so that all have a chance to hit overheads. Play to fifteen.

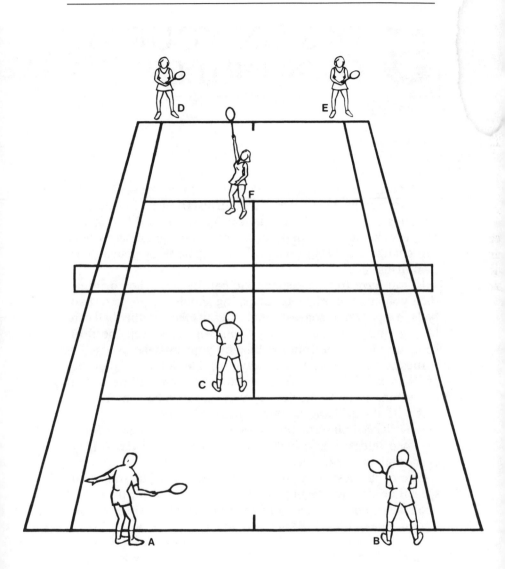

Lob Game

5 DESIGN YOUR OWN DRILLS

The drills in this book are the result of many years of coaching and playing experience. These drills are used by some of America's finest players, but they can also be used by players of every skill level. To make drilling fit your special needs, you can change the rules of the drills in this book or design your own drills.

If you have trouble keeping the ball in play when drilling, then you and the others participating should keep one or two balls in a pocket. If someone makes a mistake, another ball can be put into play immediately. This will help keep the drill going and keep you from dwelling on your mistakes.

Inexperienced players may have trouble doing some of the drills as explained. In most cases, this problem will be solved by moving closer to the net. They should then have more success with the drill and maintain interest longer.

Experienced players sometimes lose intensity when drilling. To keep intensity at a high level, players should try to play every ball on one bounce.

One of the best ways to make sure that drills fit your own special needs is to design your own drills. Use the drills in this book as a guide when designing your own. They will give you a good idea of how drills are developed.

To design your own drill, you need to start with a goal for the drill. Decide what aspect of the game you would like to work on and then use your creativity to invent a suitable drill. For example, if you have difficulty hitting backhand volleys, then your drill should be designed around that part of your game. To improve your backhand volley, you may want to design a technique drill similar to the crosscourt volley drills found in chapter one.

You can practice the same shot in a game situation by using a serve and return drill. Follow your serve to the net and have your practice partner hit all the returns to your backhand. You could play out the point or stop after the first volley, but in any case, your partner should try to hit all the balls to your backhand side.

There is no limit to the number and variety of drills you can design. There are an endless number of situations that occur when playing tennis, and you can design a drill around each situation. To help you develop your own drills, a few blank drill sheets are included starting on page 170.

You can get a firsthand look at how drills are developed by attending a workshop sponsored by the USTA. These workshops are conducted throughout the country and are conveniently scheduled. Many of the coaches who submitted drills for this book are frequent speakers at the USTA Tennis Workshops. For more information write:

USTA Workshops
USTA Education Research Center
729 Alexander Road
Princeton, NJ 08540
(or call 609-452-2580)

Good luck and have fun with your drills.

USTA SERVICES AND PUBLICATIONS

If you are a recreation leader, teaching professional, or tennis enthusiast, you should be aware that the United States Tennis Association provides a variety of services to the tennis playing public:

• The USTA Information Department can answer tennis-related questions ranging from how to build a tennis court to how to call the lines in a match without an umpire.
• The USTA National Film Library contains the latest tennis films and videocassettes available for rent.
• The USTA Publications Department offers a comprehensive selection of excellent tennis publications.
• Seed Money Grants are available to assist community leaders in the formation of new programs.
• The USTA Racket Donation Program provides equipment to schools and parks that cannot afford to purchase equipment or that serve students who cannot afford rackets.
• The USTA Clinicians Service provides experienced coaches and teachers to help initiate programs.
• The USTA sponsors regional and national seminars and meetings devoted to recreational tennis, fund raising, and other topics of interest to teaching professionals and local community leaders.

USTA Publications

These references are among the books and publications available from the USTA Publications Department. They are just a few of the more than one hundred titles and program aids available from the USTA. You can get a free publication

163

catalog as well as more information on the many services and programs offered by the USTA by writing: Publications Department, USTA Education and Research Center, 729 Alexander Road, Princeton, NJ 08540, or calling 609-452-2580.

Rules of Tennis and Cases and Decisions. The official rules of the International Tennis Federation.

Illustrated Introduction to the Rules of Tennis. A summary of the rules and code of tennis in simplified language and with appealing illustrations. Recommended for beginning players from eight to eighty.

The Code. Rules, principles, and guidelines which apply in any match conducted without officials.

A Friend at Court. Includes the Rules of Tennis and Cases and Decisions, The Code, USTA Tournament Regulations, and officiating techniques and tactics.

USTA Schools Program Tennis Curriculum. The United States Tennis Association's step-by-step guide to teaching tennis in the schools. The USTA Schools Program is specifically geared to giving all young Americans the opportunity to experience the lifetime benefits of tennis. The USTA Schools Program Curriculum is a vital component of this program. Each of the twenty-four lessons is designed to accommodate a large number of students in either a gymnasium or a schoolyard. Each twenty-five- to thirty-minute lesson covers a specific tennis topic. Each contains a statement of needed equipment, a summary of the lesson's aim and performance objectives, and the recommended procedures and activities.

USTA Courtstar Program (kit) An on-court program package for beginner instruction. Organized into a compact kit, Courtstar is designed especially for group teaching in schools, parks, and community centers. Each kit contains preplanned agendas with complimentary posters, leadership texts, and class roll forms, as well as iron-ons and test cards for ten students. For classes larger than ten, additional student materials may be ordered.

USTA Starter Tennis (kit) An elementary instructional program developed by the USTA especially for use by groups with limited facilities. Starter Tennis can be taught in a gym, on a blacktop, or against a wall. Each Starter Tennis package includes a teacher's guide, and booklets, skill tests, certificates, and badges for twenty-five students.

USTA Sportstar (kit) A complete program for establishing a positive attitude toward tennis rules, conduct, and competition. Sportstar was designed to make the teaching of sportsmanship a rewarding and pleasant process for teachers and coaches. Recommended for players in grade school through high school, Sportstar has a message for players of all ages: that "how you play the game" is more than a matter of technical proficiency. Each kit contains everything instructors will need to help develop lasting traits of good sportsmanship in their students.

The National Tennis Rating Program (kit) Contains everything needed to organize and conduct an effective on-court NTRP clinic. Included in the kit are an attractive poster, sample press release to announce the clinic, a guide to the NTRP, and multiple copies of the NTRP brochure. An excellent tool for those wanting to use the National Tennis Rating Program in activities for their club or organization.

USTA Senior Recreational Doubles (kit) A program package for tennis leaders that provides tennis play for men and women age fifty and over and self-rated 3.0 or below on the NTRP scale. Senior Doubles uses a round robin format in progressive doubles so that any number of people can play. Each kit contains warm-up and promotional posters, individual player record cards, coordinator's instruction sheet and record, award certificates, and enough player materials for twenty participants.

BIBLIOGRAPHY

These publications are available from the USTA Publications Department and bookstores.

Anthony, Julie, and Nick Bollettieri. *A Winning Combination.* New York: Charles Scribner's Sons, 1980.

Bollettieri, Nick, and Barry McDermott. *Nick Bollettieri's Junior Tennis.* New York: Simon and Schuster, 1984.

Braden, Vic, and Bill Bruns. *Vic Braden's Tennis for the Future.* Boston: Little, Brown and Co., 1977.

Groppel, Jack L. *Tennis for Advanced Players and Those Who Would Like to Be.* Champaign, Ill.: Human Kinetics Publishers, Inc., 1984.

LaMarche, Robert J. *Tennis Basics.* Englewood Cliffs, N.J.: Prentice-Hall, Inc., 1983.

Loehr, Dr. James. *Athletic Excellence—Mental Toughness Training for Sports.* Denver: Forum Publishing Company, 1982.

MacCurdy, Doug, and Shawn Tully. *Sports Illustrated Tennis.* New York: Harper and Row, 1980.

Meinhardt, Tom, and Jim Brown. *Tennis Group Instruction II.* Reston, Va.: AAHPERD, 1984.

Navratilova, Martina, with Mary Carillo. *Tennis My Way.* New York: Charles Scribner's Sons, 1983.

Seixas, Jr., Vic, and Joel Cohen. *Prime Time Tennis.* New York: Charles Scribner's Sons, 1983.

United States Professional Tennis Association. *Tennis: A Professional Guide.* Tokyo: Kodansha International, 1984.

Van Der Meer, Dennis. *Dennis Van Der Meer's Complete Book of Tennis.* New York: Simon and Schuster, 1982.

CONTRIBUTORS

DAVID BENJAMIN is director of racket sports and men's tennis coach at Princeton University. During his ten-year tenure, Princeton netmen have won seven Eastern Collegiate Athletic Conference Division I Fall Classic titles, six Eastern Intercollegiate Tennis Association Championships, and national rankings in seven out of nine seasons. David is president and executive director of the Intercollegiate Tennis Coaches Association (ITCA), chairman of the NCAA Tennis committee, and chairman of the Prince–Nike National Indoor Intercollegiate Singles and Doubles Championship Tournaments. David is the author of *Competitive Tennis: A Guide for Parents and Young Players*.

NICK BOLLETTIERI is director of the Nick Bollettieri Tennis Academy in Brandenton, Florida, and the Nick Bollettieri Tennis Camp at Wayland Academy in Beaver Dam, Wisconsin. Nick has been active in tennis camps, resorts, and schools for over twenty-five years. His tennis academy is a boarding facility where students attend academic classes at nearby schools in the morning and participate in intensive tennis training programs in the afternoon. Nick's coaching successes include 1983 U.S. Open semifinalist Jimmy Arias, Brian Gottfried, Mike DePalmer, Aaron Krickstein, and Carling Bassett. Nick is an instruction editor for *World Tennis* and has authored *A Winning Combination, Tennis Your Way,* and *Nick Bollettieri's Junior Tennis*.

GAYLE GODWIN is the head coach of the UCLA Bruins women's tennis team. She is a graduate of UCLA, having played there from 1969 to 1973. As a senior, she captured the Pacific-8 and All-Cal doubles championships. After her graduation, she continued her playing career on the Southern Clay Court and Eastern Grass Court Circuits in 1974 to 1975 while serving as captain and coach of the National Wightman Cup

Team. In 1979, she coached the U.S. Women's Team in the Pan American Games. She held the position of coach of the British Petroleum Cup Team from 1978–1980 and has coached the USTA Junior Federation Cup team since 1974. Gayle was also coach of the USA Women's Olympic Tennis Team at the 1984 Los Angeles Olympic Games.

CHUCK KRIESE is the tennis coach at Clemson University, where his overall record is 222–97. Chuck has been acknowledged as the builder of a tennis powerhouse at Clemson. Clemson has gone to the NCAA national tournament every year since 1978. Additionally, Clemson has been ranked in the top fifteen in the nation since 1978. Chuck is the founder and director of the Clemson Tiger Tennis Camp and Tennis Excellence, Inc., a junior training program for South Carolina youths. In 1981, Chuck was named Coach of the Year by both the ITCA and the United States Professional Tennis Association.

ANN LEBEDEFF is an adjunct assistant professor and the women's tennis coach at the University of Arizona. Her teams have finished in the top twenty in the nation since 1979. Ann is a former National Women's Intercollegiate doubles champion and a member of the U.S. Junior Wightman Cup team. Her major tournament wins include two singles and one doubles titles on the American Express Challenger's Circuit in 1976, and the Washington State Open singles title and Pacific Northwest doubles championship in 1975.

DOUG MACCURDY is the director of development for the International Tennis Federation. He is based in London but travels worldwide, working closely with the national associations to further the development of the game. Doug has worked with the USTA as administrator of the USTA International Project and as coordinator of the USTA Clinicians Service. He served as technical advisor to the popular television series "Play Your Best Tennis" and coauthored *Sports Illustrated Tennis*. Doug was also the director of instruction at the Lawrenceville Tennis Camp in New Jersey from 1973 to 1984.

STEVE STEFANKI is the captain-coach of the USTA Men's Junior Davis Cup Team. In this capacity, he travels the Grand Prix circuit each summer with a select group of top collegiate players. He owns a teaching facility in the Napa Valley, where he works with ranked juniors. A graduate of the University of California, he was their number one singles and doubles player and captain in 1972. In 1983, he coached the U.S. team at the Pan American Games. Steve also served as coach for the USA Men's Olympic Tennis Team at the 1984 Los Angeles Olympic Games.

LARRY TABAK is coordinator of the USTA Schools Program and the USTA Programs for the Disabled. His duties focus on implementing national programs, serving as an in-house journalist for the USTA Education and Research Center, and conducting clinics for a wide variety of promotions and training seminars. He is also the staff liaison for the USTA Sports Medicine Committee and has spearheaded the USTA's involvement with local and state chapters of the Special Olympics across the country. Prior to joining the USTA staff, Larry, a member of the USPTA, helped initiate tennis programs at clubs in Iowa and Southern California. As a free-lance writer, Larry has been a regular contributor to regional and national publications since 1978.

BLANK DRILL SHEETS

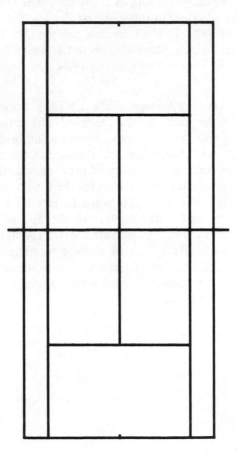

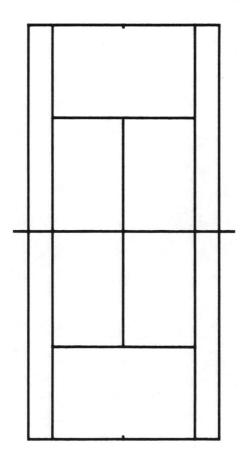

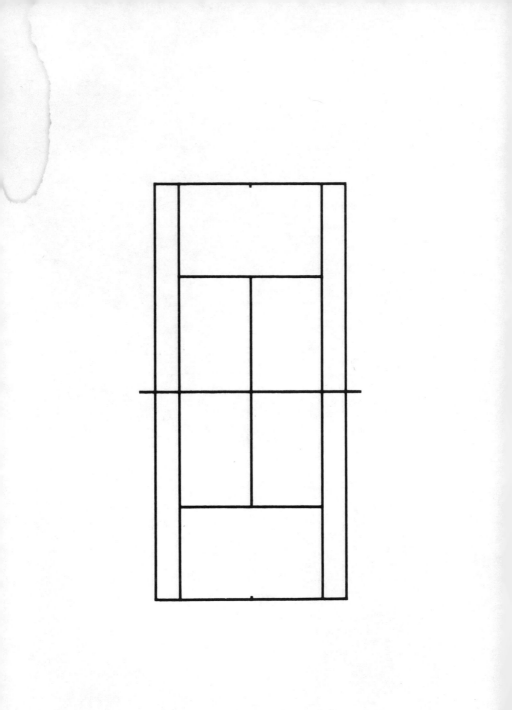

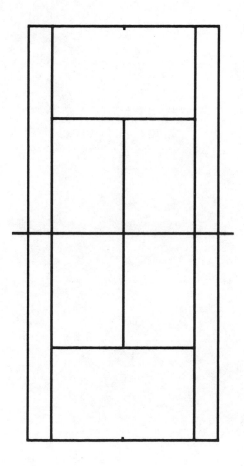

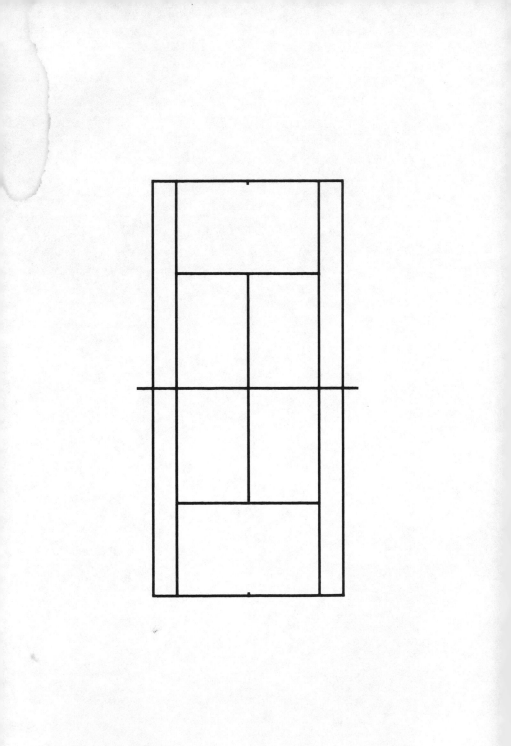

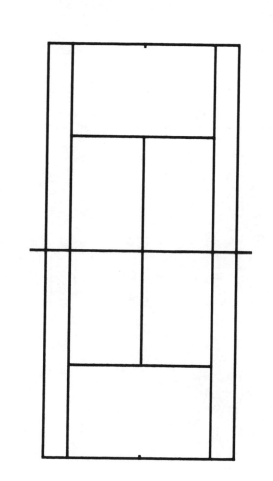

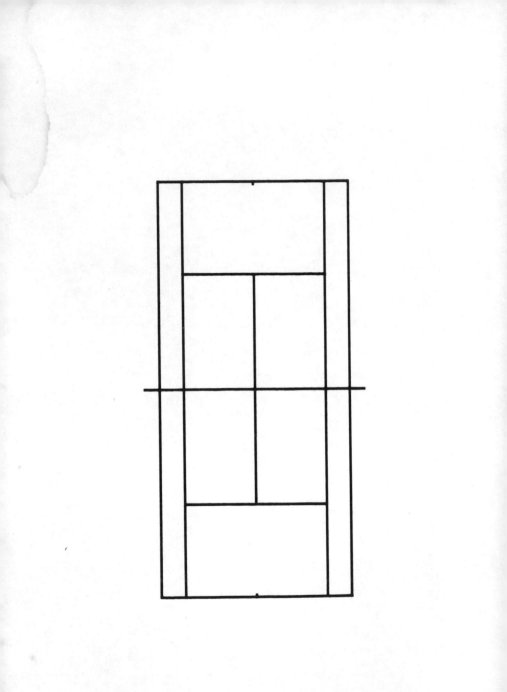

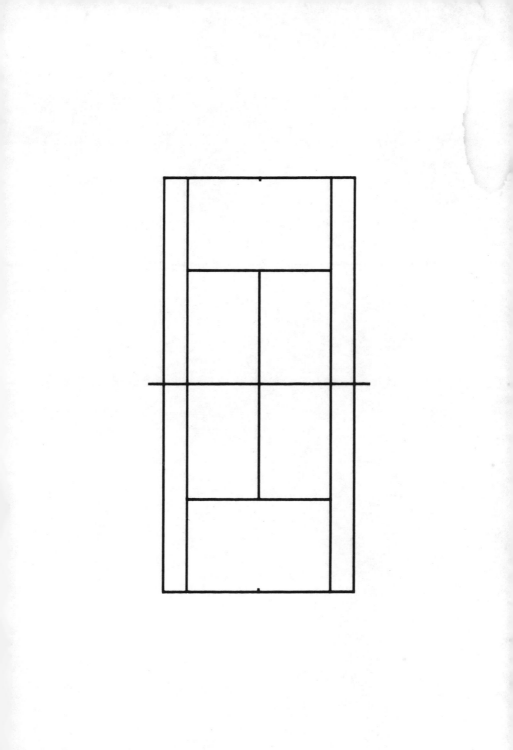

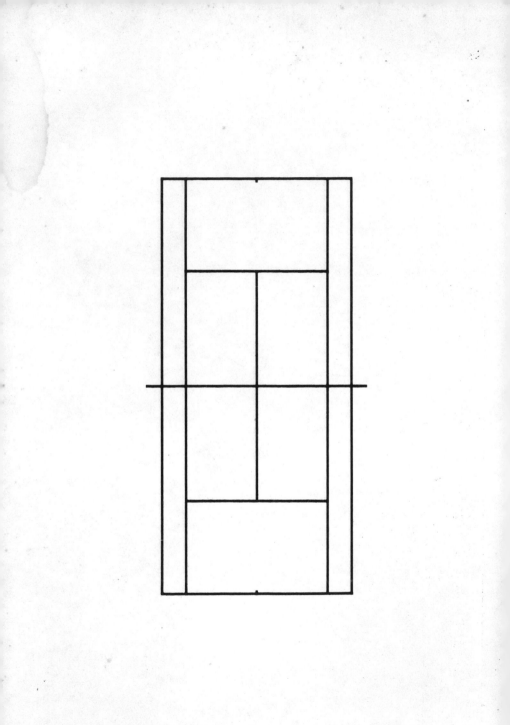